Cancer

A POSITIVE APPROACH

Cancer

A POSITIVE APPROACH

Dr Hilary Thomas
& Professor Karol Sikora

Thorsons
An Imprint of HarperCollins*Publishers*

Thorsons
An Imprint of HarperCollins*Publishers*
77–85 Fulham Palace Road,
Hammersmith, London W6 8JB
1160 Battery Street,
San Francisco, California 94111–1213

Published by Thorsons 1995

1 3 5 7 9 10 8 6 4 2

© Dr Hilary Thomas & Professor Karol Sikora 1995

Dr Hilary Thomas & Professor Karol Sikora assert the moral right to
be identified as the authors of this work

A catalogue record for this book is available from the British Library

ISBN 0 7225 3132 X

Printed in Great Britain by HarperCollinsManufacturing Glasgow

Contents

Acknowledgements   vii
Foreword   ix

SECTION 1: CANCER ITSELF   1
1 What Is Cancer?   3
2 What Causes Cancer?   16
3 Diagnosing Cancer   61

SECTION 2: TREATMENT   69
4 The System and How It Functions   71
5 Surgery   82
6 Radiotherapy   92
7 Chemotherapy   111
8 Hormone Therapy   131

SECTION 3: COPING WITH CANCER   135
9 Complementary Medicine   137
10 After Treatment   156
11 Controversies in Cancer   176
12 The Future   185

Useful Information   216
Further Reading   221
Glossary   223
Index   225

Acknowledgements

We are grateful to our patients for the incentive to write this book. It is our response to requests for more information about their disease, its treatment and their outlook. We hope that it fulfils their expectations. We are indebted to Gill Miller for her diligent, undaunted efforts with the manuscript. Thanks are also due to Jane Judd, Sarah Sutton, Wanda Whiteley and Maureen Thomas for their faith in this project, and to our families for their tolerance, without which this book might not have seen the light of day.

Foreword

For most people, cancer is a huge fear, the great unknown. 'The Big C', they sometimes call it, in a misleading throwback to the days when cure rates and treatments for many of the 200 or so different types of cancer were a pale shadow of what they are now. Misunderstandings, myths and ignorance, passed down from generation to generation, die hard. This splendid new book by two acknowledged cancer experts from London's Hammersmith Hospital – Hilary Thomas and Karol Sikora – finally and firmly lays them to rest. The mystique and uncertainties are swept aside, and in their place is painted a direct, realistic and honest picture that will be of enormous benefit to the growing number of people who have – or will develop – cancer.

This book will not remove the entire bewildering mix of emotions that accompany a diagnosis of cancer, but it will ensure that they are tamed by a firm and clear bedrock of understanding which busy doctors and consultants often do not have the time to provide. On top of this, room has also been found to provide details and contact points of the many organizations that offer a wide range of specialist help and support.

Karol Sikora has been instrumental in highlighting inconsistencies in the quality of treatment for cancer patients across the United Kingdom. Hilary Thomas is a well-known specialist in the field of gynaecological oncology. Their understanding of patients' needs, set against the background of commitment and practical experience with a wide variety of patients, has produced a book which satisfies a long-standing need. None of us can safely predict that we will not walk into a doctor's surgery tomorrow, next month or next year to be told that we have cancer. Now – at last – everyone can be prepared for that possible diagnosis with a full understanding of what is involved. *Cancer – a Positive Approach* is clearly essential reading, not only for cancer patients – present and future – but for all who love and care for them as well.

Martyn Lewis

Cancer Itself

CHAPTER ONE

What Is Cancer?

C ancer is a common problem. One in three of us will develop it. By the year 2010 this number will be one in two. We read about it daily in newspapers and magazines. It seems to be all around us gathering momentum. Even in the 1990s, when much is taken for granted about the power of modern medicine, the association between cancer and death is so strong that the topic can still be thought of as taboo. It is a myth that everyone with cancer will eventually die from it. Many people, particularly if the disease is diagnosed at an early stage, make a complete recovery. Indeed, the death rate for many chronic medical conditions such as heart disease is far greater than that for cancer.

Moreover, in the last 20 years there have been dramatic strides in our understanding of what cancer is and how best to treat it. Cancers that were almost universally fatal in the past, such as Hodgkin's disease and testicular cancer, are nearly completely curable now. There have been tremendous improvements in the care of all cancer patients, from making the diagnosis with greater precision to following what is happening during treatment and controlling any unpleasant symptoms. We have much better information about the numbers and sort of people it is likely to affect. It is true that the disease is becoming more common. This is not because of change in our environment, it is just that we live longer as a population and, as cancer occurs more commonly in the elderly, the incidence is bound to go up.

We have also managed to break through some of the taboos that used to surround cancer, so the diagnosis is quite open between doctor and patient and between family and friends. But this new frankness means that the need for information has never been greater. Consumerism has hit health care in a big way. The way health services around the world are adapting to dealing with the spiralling costs of high technology may demonstrate that no society has the perfect answer. If consumerism is used correctly it can change the way we live and the quality of our health care for the better, but to avoid tilting at windmills it must be based on facts. Here we provide an unbiased guide to the world of cancer and its treatment. A greater understanding will dispel many myths and show the promising path forward.

THE CELL

To understand what cancer is, we must look at how our body is made. We are all built of cells so tiny that they are only visible by means of a powerful microscope. About one thousand billion are needed to make a person. The cells of different tissues are specialized to have different functions. A muscle cell, for example, has tiny molecular ropes to allow it to contract; a skin cell has a tough waterproof coat to protect it from the environment, and a liver cell is a little chemical refinery continuously cleaning the blood of potential poisons. In most people these different cells work in perfect harmony, but sometimes things go wrong. If a single cell dies, one of its many identical partners simply takes over its job. If we cut ourselves, then a whole series of repair processes are brought into action. Cells start to divide and they readily replace damaged tissue. Normal cells are dying all the time in our bodies, to be replaced by new and healthy ones, but if a cell starts to grow and divide in an abnormal way, so getting out of control, then problems can arise. Sometimes this leads to cancer, a disease of abnormal growth. To understand the basic problem we have to look first at how normal cells grow and reproduce.

NORMAL CELL STRUCTURE AND GROWTH

Normal cells consist of a membrane, cytoplasm and a nucleus (*see Fig. 1.1*). The membrane is a complex structure which includes a large number of protein molecules stretching across it. These project an external portion, which acts as a receptor, and an internal portion. Signals received by the external part are transmitted through the membrane to tell the cell what to do. When we are suddenly frightened, for example, adrenalin in released into the bloodstream. The cell receptors pick this up and prepare our muscles and nervous system to deal rapidly with the situation. Cell surface markers also enable the body's immune system to recognize foreign molecules of infected cells, processes which are vital in resisting and overcoming infection. In addition, the cell membrane provides a skeleton for the cell and helps to maintain the correct balance of chemicals inside.

The cytoplasm is the biological soup inside the cell which contains structures vital for the working and growth of the cell. These are essential for the division into two daughter cells during growth and for the production of substances by the cell as part of its everyday function.

The control plant of the cell is the nucleus. This contains material known as DNA (deoxyribonucleic acid) – a chemical sequence in which information is stored and passed on from one cell to the next, and indeed from one generation to the next. It is this information which determines whether, for example, a cell will be part of muscle or skin. It is also through the DNA that physical characteristics – height, colour of hair and eyes, intelligence and so on – are passed on from parents to children.

All complex organisms, including man, grow from a single cell by a series of events in which a cell splits into two – a process known as mitosis. During this the DNA and the nucleus of a single cell replicates itself to form two nuclei. At the same time the cytoplasm divides and surrounds the two new nuclei, resulting in two cells each enclosed by a membrane. The two new cells

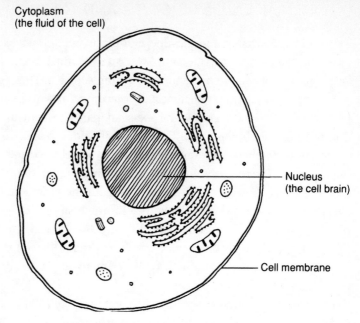

Cytoplasm
(the fluid of the cell)

Nucleus
(the cell brain)

Cell membrane

Figure 1.1 A normal cell.

(daughter cells of the original) then divide to form four cells, and so on.

Sometimes, however, this growth process can go wrong. For reasons not fully understood, part of the information carried in the DNA becomes altered and an abnormal cell is formed. This process is called malignant transformation, and it is the key to understanding cancer. The abnormal cell continues to divide, even though it is receiving no signals to do so from the organism. A cluster of abnormal cells forms a tumour which can grow and spread.

Normal cells do not become malignant suddenly. There is a series of events which culminates in a cell growing out of control. These events take place long before the cancer becomes a problem. We know this because sometimes, purely by chance, some of the earlier changes can be seen. In the cells lining the small airways of the lung, little areas of change can be detected by looking at cells down a microscope. These changes are much more common in heavy smokers, who we know have a much greater chance of getting lung cancer. Such cells may divide faster, look abnormal, and arrange themselves in a disorderly fashion.

THE MAIN COMPONENTS OF A CELL ARE …

- *the cell membrane – its outer coat*

- *the cytoplasm – a gelatinous soup*

- *its nucleus – the cell's 'brain'*

TUMOURS

A tumour is a mass of tissue formed as a result of cells growing abnormally and excessively. These cells continue to grow indefinitely and without restraint. Tumour basically means a swelling. There are two types – benign and malignant. Broadly speaking, benign tumours are localized – that is they do not spread from the part of the body in which they began. They often have a clear capsule, a rim of normal tissue which marks the limit of the tumour. They may be detected, because as they grow they press on other important structures in the body, such as blood vessels or the intestines. In the skin they cause blemishes which can easily be seen. A simple wart is a good example of a benign tumour. On the whole, such tumours are easily removed by surgery and do not recur. It is only in rare cases – for example, if a benign tumour exists deep in a vital part of the brain where surgery is likely to cause serious damage – that this is impossible.

Malignant tumours are true cancers. They are virtually never surrounded by a capsule and will often erode adjacent tissues, infiltrating other parts of the body and extending with crab-like projections in all directions. Indeed, when cancer was first described it was named after the Latin for a crab. With a few exceptions, the unequivocal feature of the malignant tumour is its ability to spread through the blood and lymph vessels and establish itself in other parts of the body. This process is called metastasis – from the two Greek words *meta*, meaning change, and *stasis*, meaning place. The cancer cells have quite simply changed places, spreading around the body from which they arose.

THE CANCER CELL

The components and structure of a cancer cell are essentially the same as those of a normal one. The most important difference is that cancer cells will continue to multiply, often outgrowing their blood supply and the space available. Most of them grow more rapidly than the normal cells from which they originated. Down the microscope, cancer cells often look very different from each other and from their normal parents, and often contain large bizarre nuclei. One reason for this is that the cells grow so quickly they have no time to organize themselves, but just keep dividing.

The most dangerous feature of malignant tumours is their ability to spread to other parts of the body where they can generate new tumours. Scientists do not yet fully understand how this happens, but the fact that cells within the same tumour can look very different from each other suggests that cancer cells continually modify their behaviour in growth. It may be that during this process bits of DNA associated with a natural tendency to spread become exaggerated. The likelihood of the tumour spreading and the rate at which this occurs vary from one type of tumour to another.

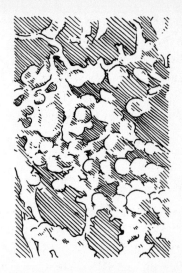

Figure 1.2 *Normal and cancer cells. The cells on the left are normal – they stop growing when they touch. The cells on the right are malignant – they are piling up and have lost their normal growth restraint. These cells are growing on a dish in the laboratory. In a patient, the cancer cells would develop into a lump, eventually spreading to other parts of the body.*

HOW DO CANCERS SPREAD?

CANCER CAN SPREAD IN SEVERAL WAYS

- *direct invasion*

- *through body cavities*

- *in the lymphatic system*

- *through blood vessels*

There are several ways in which cancer can spread. Cancer cells can pass into the lymph channels. These are tiny pipes connecting the lymph nodes in all parts of the body, ultimately draining into a large vein. You can feel normal lymph nodes in the neck quite easily. They are usually pea-sized. Sometimes they swell after a throat infection. This is part of the body's normal immune response. The spread of cancer often follows the natural routes of lymph drainage of the area from which it arises – so breast cancer cells spread into the nodes under the armpit.

The bloodstream can also convey malignant fragments to distant parts. The lungs and liver act as huge filters of the bloodstream, and they are often sites for secondary cancer growth. Cells can also seed directly in body cavities, such as the peritoneum, within the abdomen, or the pleura, the lining around the lungs. Here, cells break off the tumour and migrate in the fluid in which they bathe. The transplantations of tumour cells may be possible along needle tracks or in the scar after an operation. A cascade of events is involved between the shedding of a single cell by the primary tumour and the disease establishing itself in another part of the body. Cancers do not spread in a haphazard or arbitrary way, and particular tumours have favoured sites. This is, to some degree, related to the roots of spread. Sarcoma (tumours arising from the body's structural tissues) often spread by showering cells into the bloodstream. Such cells are filtered by the small blood vessels in the lungs, so secondary tumours in this area are common. Prostate cancer likes to grow in bone, often in the spine or pelvis. There must be some factor in the bones of this area that encourages the growth of the prostate cancer cells. Colon cancer often colonizes the liver, causing damage and eventually a reduction in the liver's ability to clear poisons from the blood.

But, although we know which sites a particular type of tumour is likely to be found in, it is less easy to predict whether or not the disease will spread in any one person. One theory for this is that the body's immune system may detect and engulf cancer cells as they travel. Another is that tumours that have begun in one part of the body may not necessarily be able to establish themselves in a different type of tissue. As yet, we do not know which factors make it possible for cancer cells to spread. An understanding of this process may be the key to curing cancer. We are already able to control, with surgery or radiation, the majority of solid localized tumours. It is cells that get away which can defeat us.

CLASSIFYING CANCER

CANCERS CAN BE CLASSIFIED BY THE TYPES OF TISSUE FROM WHICH THEY ARISE

- *carcinoma*

- *epithelial tissue – e.g. breast, lung, colon, skin*

- *sarcoma*

- *connective tissue – e.g. bone, muscle*

- *lymphoma*

- *lymphoid tissue*

- *leukaemia*

- *white blood cells in the bone marrow*

Cancer can occur in any organ of the body. The behaviour pattern of different cancers varies enormously. There are currently over 200 classifiable sites at which tumours can arise, and many of these can be broken down into further subtypes. This reflects the many different cells that go to make up the human body – many of which can evolve to grow out of control.

Tumours are classified by the site at which they originate. For example, a patient with breast cancer that has spread through the bloodstream to the liver is said to have metastatic breast cancer (i.e. breast cancer that has spread) and not a primary liver tumour.

This classification by likely site of origin often causes confusion to patients and families. Tumours may also be given a name reflecting the type of structure from which they come. A carcinoma, for example, comes from cells lining the body's cavities. Such cells are found in the lung, colon, breast and in many other organs. Carcinomas are by far and away the commonest type. Tumours arising from the body's structural tissues – muscle, tendon, bone and cartilage – are called sarcomas. Those arising from the lymphatic system are called lymphomas; and cancers of the white blood cell and bone marrow, leukaemias.

SYMPTOMS OF CANCER

Because there are many different types of cancer there is no one way in which it first draws attention to itself. What happens first depends on the site and size of the tumour, on any spread of the disease, as well as on any other medical problems a patient may have. For example, a small tumour on the vocal cord will rapidly create an ulcer. This prevents the complete closure of the vocal cord while speaking, and leads to hoarseness. In this way a relatively tiny tumour produces the alarming symptom of persistent hoarseness, driving the patient to the doctor rather quickly, usually before the tumour has had time to spread. Patients with lung cancer, on the other hand, often show no unusual symptoms until relatively late. The majority of such patients are smokers who are used to frequent coughing, shortness of breath and even occasional chest pains – all features of a growing tumour. By the time something really novel develops, such as the coughing up of a small amount of blood, the tumour has firmly established itself. Pain comes from the pressure on, or the destruction of, tissues containing nerve fibre endings. The centres of most organs contain no nerve endings, and it is only when that outer lining is stretched that the patient notices there is something wrong.

Being aware of symptoms which may well be because of cancer

is an important part of health education. An organ not functioning properly is one symptom. There are many others that are much less specific. These include a feeling of tiredness, weakness, weight loss, fever, nausea and sweating at night. How these effects are produced is not always clear. The most likely explanation is that substances are released by tumour cells which trigger the symptoms indirectly. Of course, any of these may be caused by medical problems other than cancer. If any unusual symptom persists you should see your doctor. In most cases it will not be because of cancer.

CANCER TREATMENT

CANCER TREATMENT

- *Surgery*

- *Radiotherapy*

- *Chemotherapy*

- *Hormonal treatment*

- *Immunotherapy*

Cancer treatment is often confusing, even to many doctors specializing in this field. The best treatment depends on a wide range of criteria – the age of the patient, whether preservation of fertility is important or possible, personal preference; and even the distance to be travelled for therapy, the type of disease, its site and degree of spread are clearly vital factors in determining which treatment is best. We will look at all these in more detail, but here is a brief summary of the methods of treatment in current use.

Surgery is likely to be used in obtaining a sample of tissue for diagnosis. In some cancers, where it is important that the bulk of disease is removed surgically, it can be the central part of treatment. Nevertheless, it is a common misconception that in the last resort cancer can be cut out. Cancer cells cannot be distinguished accurately with the naked eye, so the surgeon cannot be completely certain all the tumour has been removed. Cells may sometimes be left behind and will soon fill the space made available by growing more rapidly.

Radiation has been used to treat cancer since its discovery nearly 100 years ago, but not all tumours are radiosensitive. Over the last few decades, increasing computerization has led to much greater accuracy in the way radiotherapy can be given, so reducing its side-effects.

Although chemotherapy (treatment with anti-cancer drugs) has been available from the latter half of this century, it is only in the past 25 years that is has seen widespread successful application. With an increasing number of types of compounds available, coupled with their decreased side-effects and costs, some tumours have become curable. The vast majority of common tumours, unfortunately, remain relatively resistant to cure by chemotherapy. Moreover, certain drugs have serious long-term side-effects. Because of a major risk of further cancer being caused, for example, certain drugs are not used in the treatment of childhood cancers. As better agents and antidotes are uncovered, side-effects such as hair loss, nausea and infections are gradually being overcome.

Hormone therapy is suitable for a limited number of hormone-sensitive tumours – notably breast and prostate cancer. If the tumour responds to hormonal adjustment it may control the spread of the disease for a number of years with little in the way of side-effects for the patient. This is particularly likely in the elderly; younger patients tend to have more aggressive tumours which are not so responsive. Hormone treatment can usually be taken in the form of simple tablets, making life easy.

There are no hard and fast rules in the treatment of cancer. Everybody is different, so it is not really surprising that when they become ill their needs will differ. The treatments available for cancer have become very sophisticated. The difficulty for the specialist is to know how best to combine them for an individual. In addition, the situation must be continually reassessed. Is the tumour responding to treatment? What are the side-effects and are they likely to limit the dose of drugs or radiation given? If so, will this reduce the chance of cure? All these questions must be constantly reviewed to achieve the best results.

THE FUTURE

Sadly, anybody and everybody can develop cancer. There is no watertight avoidance strategy. There are some general principles suggested in the next chapter, so it is sensible to follow these. Individuals who have a strong family history of cancer are more at risk, particularly with inherited cancers or those where there is a strong inherited trait (such as breast, colon and ovarian cancer). In these situations members of the family can be screened regularly. As further advances occur, it should be possible to detect malignancies at a very early stage without resorting to surgery.

Although statistics tell us that cancer is becoming more common, many cancers related to unhealthy habits – for example, smoking-related lung cancers in men – are on the decline. What has altered is our ability to detect cancer at an earlier treatable stage. Although tumours have been seen in Egyptian mummies, they may not always have been diagnosed as cancer at the time. Cancer will be with us for many years to come. As we probe deeper and deeper into how cells grow and divide, we are getting down to the building blocks of life itself. It is here that the answer to cancer must lie. As we increase our understanding we will almost surely discover new methods or diagnosing, treating and ultimately preventing this important problem.

What Causes Cancer?

The most common question asked by a patient who has been found to have cancer is 'What caused it?' A tremendous amount of research has taken place over the last century to address this issue. The first clear-cut observation was made by a surgeon at St Bartholomew's Hospital in London in the eighteenth century. Percival Pott noted that chimney sweeps were prone to develop tumours of the skin surrounding the testicles. These poor boys were sent up chimneys at an early age and seldom got a wash. The various chemicals and soot accumulated in their groins and caused long-standing skin irritation, which eventually became malignant.

This was the first recognized example of an occupational cancer. Many others became apparent in this century: asbestos workers developing tumours in the lining around the lungs; uranium miners getting lung cancer; workers in the rubber industry, those making car tyres using aniline dyes, developing bladder cancer. Some cancers were shown to have a clear-cut single cause. Does all cancer have a specific cause, or is it the inter-relationship between many different factors that leads to cancer? The answer is not straightforward. Many factors can trigger-off the disease, but it is very difficult to disentangle which factors are important in the development of an individual patient's cancer. To understand the complexity of the situation the concept of probability must be introduced.

If you travel on an aeroplane, there is a small but definite risk that it will crash. One of the reasons for this is that the engines may fail. Let's say that the aeroplane has four jet engines, like a Boeing 747 – the common jumbo jet. The chances of one engine failing are very small. But if, for example, fire breaks out in the far right engine, the pilot can extinguish the fire and still fly on three engines. Now, one of the other engines suddenly develops vibration and stops. The pilot can still fly on two engines, although the journey becomes a bit more uncomfortable, and manoeuvring is more difficult. Then, suddenly, the third engine blows. The plane, while still able to hold its height, is unstable and very difficult to manoeuvre. A great strain is placed on that last engine. The chances of crashing now are much greater than they were at the start of the flight. If the last engine goes, then that's it. The longer the plane flies, the more chance that the engines are going to fail. If the plane continues going round the world, eventually something will go.

The best way to think of cancer is as a series of engine failures in the growth control apparatus of the cell. Many of us may well be walking around with one or two cells already on the road to cancer, but as yet no tumour has emerged. It needs several hits on the right targets within the DNA inside the cell's nucleus to cause cancer. If we stick with our aeroplane analogy, there are many factors that can cause engine failure but of course the final straw is the last engine, and that may not always pack up.

Time is often said to be the greatest enemy. In the development of cancer age is a major factor. Continuing our jumbo jet analogy, the chances of things going wrong increase with time as we fly. Similarly the chances of a cell going astray in our bodies increase as we travel on our journey through life. There are certain exceptions to this – childhood tumours, leukaemias, brain and kidney tumours may occur even in newborn babies. Testicular cancer peaks in men in their 20s and 30s, again suggesting that the events that lead to them occurred during early adolescence, or even before. But the vast majority of common tumours occur in the fifth and sixth decade of life, and increase in incidence subsequently.

This bears out the multi-hit theory: the fact that certain events have to take place for most tumours to arise.

As the population ages as a whole, because of better medical care and fewer deaths from heart disease and strokes, the incidence of cancer rises. By the year 2010 it is predicted that in most Western countries one in two people will develop cancer. This is a rather depressing statistic.

Much as we would like to, we cannot stop time and therefore the ageing process. What we can do is identify those factors in our lifestyle which may increase our cancer risk and do something about them. This chapter contains summary boxes telling you exactly how to assess your cancer risk and what to do about it.

CANCER IN THE FAMILY

We all have different faces, body-sizes and shapes, intelligence, characters and fingerprints. Underneath what we can see, we each possess our own molecular sequences of DNA. It is this sequence, the code of life, that determines our make up. Of course, the environment – physical and psychological – impinges on us, but it is the genetic material that codes for the physical machine. On the whole, patients with cancer can be reassured that the disease is not hereditary and their children are not at greater risk of getting it. But, for reasons that we do not fully understand, some of us may well be more susceptible to develop specific cancers than others. The recent rapid advances in understanding how various genes work have led to considerable interest in the genetic prediction of cancer risk. This whole area is often misunderstood by many doctors and is rapidly changing, and it is likely that within the next 10 years there will be specific tests available which will predict reliably the risk of getting certain cancers. If the risk is high then, clearly, close screening will be indicated.

There are certain very rare tumours which do behave in a classical genetic way. Retinoblastoma, a very unusual eye tumour in the retina at the back of the eye, often behaves according to strict genetic rules. The genes are carried from father to son and from mother to daughter, resulting in a nearly 50 per cent chance of retinoblastoma in the offspring. Children of such families, which fortunately are very rare, are screened from an early age to look for eye tumours, and the disease can now be cured by early surgery and radiotherapy.

Breast cancer is very common, with 1 in 12 women in Britain developing the disease. The incidence is almost one in two in certain families, and here it often occurs in both breasts, behaves aggressively and develops at an early age, sometimes under the age of 40. Although the disease is not passed on by strict genetic rules, the tendency to develop it clearly runs in the family. Screening such families to pick up tumours early may be of great value and increases the chances of successful treatment. Recently two genes called the *BRCA1* and *BRCA2* have been cloned. This means that their sequences have been identified and have been changed in the family background in certain ways. They carry a considerably increased risk of breast cancer for that family. Certain types of change in *BRCA1* can be predicted to cause cancer in 90 per cent of women before they reach the age of 70. As our knowledge of the sequence of human DNA progresses over the next decade it is likely that other, perhaps more common, cancer genes will be identified for breast and other cancers. These will be incorporated into the screening programmes we already have. Such programmes are now targetted at the high-risk groups.

Colon cancer often runs in families. There is another benign condition called familial adenomatous polyposis which is also inherited and carries an increased risk of cancer developing from the benign polyps that arise. Screening by colonoscopy – the examination of the rectum and colon using a flexible telescope – greatly reduces the risk of death from colon cancer in these patients.

There are other examples of families where there is a much higher incidence of cancer than expected. These families may have difficulty in repairing damage to DNA caused by chemical and physical agents. Alternatively, their genes may be very sensitive to such agents. In either case the risk of developing cancer is higher than normal.

We can all be reassured that the vast majority of cancers are not hereditary, and even if a close relative has had the disease you are at no greater risk of developing it. To recap: those rare cancers which may be hereditary include retinoblastoma, childhood kidney cancer (Wilm's tumour) and, in some cases, breast, ovarian and colon cancer. Clearly you cannot choose your family, so the most positive step you can take is to be aware of any potential risk and look out for possible symptoms. If a close relative of yours has had one of these cancers, ask your doctor about screening programmes – that is, regular check-ups – so that if you do develop symptoms they can be detected and treated at an early stage.

Early detection is an essential part of cancer prevention, and all women – not just those with a family history of breast cancer – should regularly check their breasts for any lumps which might indicate a tumour. Most breast lumps are completely harmless, but even those which are cancerous can be treated successfully.

REDUCING CANCER RISK

- *Make a list of your family, starting with your grandparents and including your father, mother, brother, sister, aunts, uncles and first cousins. Mark any that have cancer and note its type. If more than two have had cancer of the same type, consult your doctor.*

- *If you think your family may be at risk of developing a rare, familial cancer (e.g. retinoblastoma or childhood kidney cancer) ask your doctor about regular screening programmes.*

- *Regular breast self-examination once a month is essential for all women, as are check-ups by your GP or local well-woman clinic.*

> • *Screening programmes are now available for breast, ovarian and colon cancers. Some are in routine use for certain age groups, others are being investigated. Ask your doctor for details.*

CHEMICALS CAUSING CANCER

The realization that chemicals cause cancer came from the early observations of Percival Pott, followed by experimental work in London (in the 1920s). A group of research workers at the Institute of Cancer Research in South Kensington were fascinated by the observation that coal tar extracts obtained from the Fulham Gas Works could cause cancer when they were painted on to the skin of mice. They began to analyse the cancer causing component of coal tar, and found that specific chemical structures were responsible. Such chemicals were called carcinogens.

Since the first discovery of carcinogens 60 years ago many chemicals have now been shown to be damaging to cells, so increasing the chance of them becoming malignant. For some chemicals the risk is very high and easily spotted. A good example are the aniline dyes used to soften rubber for making tyres. It became very clear that people working in the manufacture of rubber materials stood a very high chance of getting bladder cancer. When aniline dyes were found to be responsible, far greater safety precautions were adopted and now there is little risk of factory workers ingesting the dye.

Asbestos, which was used for pipe lagging and in ship building, causes a very rare type of cancer of the membrane of the lining of the lung. This cancer, called mesothelioma, is extremely rare except in those who have been exposed to asbestos dust for long periods of time. Now rigid safety precautions are taken by those handling asbestos, including the use of special filter masks to prevent the fibres being breathed in. Asbestos is found in many old buildings, so when conversion work is done, the area is sealed off by polythene sheeting. You may have noticed this, together with danger signs about asbestos, in building work.

There are many chemicals which are now known to cause cancer. Pollution from factories and increased use of very potent chemicals in modern farming increases the chances of our exposure to them, but because we are usually exposed at only a low dose and for only a short period of time the chances of getting cancer are relatively low. It is unlikely that pollution owes more than a fraction of a percentage to our overall cancer risk and, despite all the concern that our food should be more organic, there is very little evidence suggesting that intensive farming has increased the risk of our developing cancer.

CIGARETTE SMOKING

The situation is very different for cigarette smoking. This is the greatest clear-cut reversible cause of lung cancer. Compounds similar to coal tar were found in cigarette smoke, and it is very surprising now to imagine that 40 years ago cigarettes were not recognized as a major cause of lung cancer. Look at any of the great old films of the 1940s and early 50s – the Bogart movies, such as *Casablanca*, perhaps the best examples. Nearly every character seems to be smoking at some stage. Even the film director uses cigarette smoke creatively in moments of greater poignancy. At the time, smoking was freely permissible in all public places in the UK – including hospitals, cinemas and London's Underground railway.

Things began to change when Richard Doll and his colleagues at Oxford began to survey patients with lung cancer and compare them with patients of similar age and sex who did not have the disease. They found that nearly all the lung cancer patients smoked heavily, whilst very few of the control group did. This observation was contested fiercely by the tobacco companies and those who had a powerful vested interest in the sale of tobacco. They suggested that there are many other factors responsible, such as the different lifestyle of smokers compared with non-smokers. There is evidence, for example, that smokers have a higher sugar intake than non-smokers.

Doll then went on to establish his now classic study on British doctors. Using a detailed questionnaire, followed up at regular intervals, he collected data on the chain-smoking habits of many GPs. A comparison was made between those who had stopped smoking and those who had continued, and a clear pattern emerged. Those doctors who had stopped smoking considerably reduced their risk of getting lung cancer. In other words, even heavy smokers can redeem themselves if they stop in time.

The growing body of evidence linking cigarettes to lung cancer and subsequently to heart disease and chronic bronchitis has finally led to a change in public opinion, with the Government banning cigarette advertising on television and elsewhere. However, the tobacco lobby has fought back. Sponsorship and advertising by the tobacco companies at many sporting events carry the suggestion of an association of cigarettes with health and physical ability, or with sexual prowess. The lobby is extremely powerful and not amenable to logic. The Chairman of Rothmans International recently stated: 'There is no evidence that cigarettes cause lung cancer.' But, gradually the tide of public opinion has turned, and smokers are now being shunned more and more. It is just not politically correct in the 90s to be seen smoking.

The realization that breathing in the exhaled smoke of others – passive smoking – can also lead to a significant increase in the incidence of cancer has resulted in public demand for smoke-free areas in transport, in leisure facilities and in the workplace. Courts can protect the right of an individual to choose whether to smoke or not. The evidence accumulating on passive smoking suggests that those who wish to continue to smoke should do so in the privacy of their own, well-ventilated (it is hoped), rooms. A good analogy would be a passenger on a transatlantic flight wishing, for fun, to switch off one of the engines just to see what happened. The rest of the passengers would be compelled to take part in this dangerous experiment.

Of course, many heavy smokers rationalize, rather like the tobacco industry. 'My grandfather smoked 50 cigarettes a day and lived until he was 80,' is a common reply from patients when attempts are made to reduce their smoking. The opposite is sometimes used: 'My mother died of lung cancer at 50 and she never smoked a single cigarette in her life.' These statements, which are often exaggerated, show the failure to understand the statistical nature of cancer as a disease. Another argument is that you have to die of something. This is true, but lung cancer does affect men and women in their 50s and 60s, well below the average age of death. It is also an unpleasant disease to have.

Stopping smoking or, better still, never starting is the single biggest way to reduce your cancer risk. Of course, it is difficult to stop completely. If you are a heavy smoker, then start by trying to cut it down. Limit your cigarette consumption to specific times of the day. Change to a low-tar brand, do not inhale the smoke, use a longer filter and milder cigarette, then make the big step: abandon smoking completely. You will be surprised how healthy you will feel a month or so later. Breathing will be easier, you will cough less and will feel fitter and more able to go about life. Many arguments against stopping smoking are put forward. OK, so you may put on a little weight as you transfer nervous activity from cigarettes to food. You may start drinking a little bit more alcohol. This does not matter in the short term because these habits, too, can be curbed later once you have given up smoking. Seek the help of your GP. He is in a good position to advise about various aids, such as nicotine patches and chewing gum. Also, there may be a local anti-smoking clinic. Such clinics can be very helpful. But, at the end of the day the decision is yours. The will-power to give up has to come from within.

If you are a non-smoker, then campaign for a no smoking environment. This will reduce the risk of your getting cancer by passive smoking and also provide an atmosphere in which smokers are shunned. How many times have you started coughing when a colleague has lit up a cigarette? Personal liberty is a grand-sounding title for the ability to poison your friends, family and workplace. Insist on a smoke-free workplace. Why should you have to put up with other people's bad habits. Recent changes in public transport laws are leading the way. The London Underground system has now abolished smoking altogether. Airlines are beginning to schedule non-smoking flights, but at the moment these are mainly confined to short domestic routes for fear of damaging potentially profitable business from international customers. However, there are some progressive airlines, such as Singapore Airlines, who are beginning to make even long-haul flights smoke-free. There is nothing worse than being a non-smoker in a plane and sitting at the boundary between smoking and non-smoking areas.

Above all, discourage children from smoking. This is the key to the future. The tobacco industry spends millions on advertising, brainwashing young people with the perceived benefits to them of cigarette smoking. The evil influence is greatest now in the Third World, where there are no restrictions on advertising. The implication in most of the campaigns is that by smoking a chosen brand of cigarette you will become important, rich, trendy and sexy. In the face of this, health education spends a paltry sum by comparison. We have to dissuade teenagers from taking up smoking. If we can, then the next generation will reap tremendous benefits.

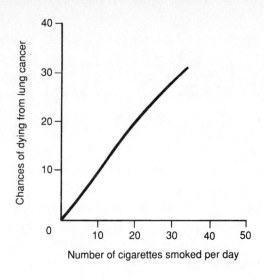

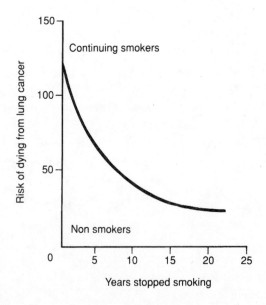

Figure 2.1 *The risk of lung cancer. The risk of lung cancer increases steadily with the number of cigarettes smoked, and starts to decrease as soon as someone stops smoking.*

REDUCING YOUR RISK

Stop smoking now!

- *One third of all cancer deaths are caused by smoking.*

- *Lung cancer causes 40,000 deaths a year in the UK – that's about 110 every day.*

- *If you smoke 20 cigarettes a day, you are 40 times more likely to get lung cancer than a non-smoker.*

- *Your risk of developing other tumours – in your liver, gall bladder, bladder or pancreas, ear, nose, throat and cervix – is also increased if you smoke.*

- *Your risk of developing cancer begins to fall as soon as you give up smoking.*

If you really can't give up immediately:

- *Cut down by allowing yourself to smoke only at certain times of the day.*

- *Change to a low-tar brand.*

- *Always use filter tips.*

- *Inhale less smoke.*

- *Ask your doctor about anti-smoking clinics and other ways of helping you to stop.*

If you are a non-smoker:

- *Campaign for a no smoking environment.*

- *Insist on a smoke-free workplace.*

- *Make a fuss – If someone asks, 'Do you mind if I smoke?' don't be afraid to say that you do mind.*

- *Discourage your children from smoking.*

DIET AND CANCER

We are what we eat. It is, therefore, not surprising that the constitution of our diet has been related to cancer incidence. But there are many misconceptions in this area.

The diet we eat today is not the one our body was designed to take. The basic problem is that our diet has become highly refined, concentrated and, of course, on occasions delicious. Man evolved as a hunter searching where he could for food, eating both plants and animals. If we could put Stone Age man in a time machine and send him for dinner at a fancy Paris restaurant or to the local fast-food burger store, not only would he find the surroundings strange, but he would find the food almost inedible. Let's just take a look at the modern hamburger, the sort children clamour for when offered a meal out. It is usually served with chips and a Cola drink or a milkshake.

The first problem is the fat content. As much as 70 per cent of the leanest looking burger may in fact consist of animal fat. For many years now it has been recognized that the incidence of breast cancer follows closely the daily average fat consumption (*see Figure 2.2*). Those countries where women have a high fat intake have a high level of the disease. The association between breast cancer and diet is not clear-cut, and efforts so far to elucidate it have not been successful. Calories, fat content and saturated fat, among other factors, have been looked at and none is clearly related to the risk of breast cancer beyond a general association with the relatively high-fat diet which we eat in the Western world. Moreover, fat dramatically increases the calorie content – something to be avoided if you are trying to keep your weight down. Preservatives will be added to the meat to keep it fresh, as will a range of colourings and 'unknown' chemicals. The burger will be grilled producing coal tar-like compounds which may be carcinogenic. The bun of the hamburger itself will be white and made from the most refined flour having very little fibre content. The chips will be coated in fat, and may well have added chemicals to increase the crispness of their outer coat. The Cola drink will contain the equivalent of 10 sugar lumps. The milkshake will be made from full-fat milk and chemical flavourings – all potentially dangerous. Having the odd fast-food meal is not a bad thing once in a while, but a diet which comprises only fast food is asking for trouble. There is evidence that the sorts of foods we eat can in the long term determine the incidence of cancer. Evidence for this comes from comparing the incidence of cancer in populations with radically different diets. In Africa, for example, the diet is mainly vegetarian with a high content of fibre. This results in the average African producing over a kilogram of stool daily in contrast to the average Westerner who produces less than 300 g. The incidence of colo-rectal cancer is very high in the West but almost non-existent in Africa. The reason for this is the short transit time in the intestine resulting from the high bulk of the African stool. The longer transit time in Westerners allows carcinogenic chemicals in our diet to sit in contact with the bowel wall. Another reason may well be the bacteria that inhabit the intestine. The rapid transit time may change the composition of organisms, some of which may not be able to produce the unpleasant carcinogens that we get in the West.

Furthermore, obesity will be a problem. This alone carries an increased cancer risk in certain areas of the body. Obesity is, of course, a health hazard in many ways other than just increasing cancer risk. Heart disease, high blood pressure, arthritis, psychological disturbances and strokes are all increased in patients with excess fat. It is not only grossly obese people who have these increased risks. If you go into any pub at a Sunday lunchtime you will find groups of men with pot bellies usually standing at the bar, drinking beer and sometimes smoking continuously. Middle-aged spread is induced by too much eating, partly caused by good home cooking, but also by drinking too many high-calorie fluids such as beer.

It is not always easy to alter your lifestyle. If you are in a group which meets regularly before Sunday lunch to drink beer in the pub, there is a lot of peer pressure to continue to do so. Asking for a tonic water instead of a pint may well be met with derision. Again, there are vested interests at stake trying to stop you adopting a sensible, healthy lifestyle. The breweries and publicans make their money by selling beer, and they do not wish to portray beer drinking as a cause of obesity. Those involved in advertising fast food in fast-food outlets clearly emphasize the healthy aspects and not the deleterious aspects of their products.

Once you see through these ploys it becomes easier to change things. Reducing weight is not as difficult as stopping smoking, mainly because you can still eat. The first thing to do is to review

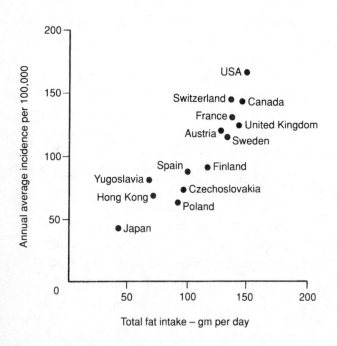

Figure 2.2 *Breast cancer related to dietary fat intake. In a study of 14 countries, the incidence of breast cancer (number of cases per 100,000 women) was found to increase in line with the average daily intake of fat.*

your behaviour patterns. Go through an average day and look at what you are eating. Take breakfast. If you have a cooked breakfast is this necessary? The standard British breakfast sold in hotels and on trains is one of the most unhealthy starts imaginable to the day. Whilst it is fun once in a while to have such a meal, every day is asking for trouble. Many people do not eat a cooked breakfast as such, but have a high-calorie intake, with fat in the form of butter, calories in the form of jams and marmalade and sugar in tea or coffee. What kind of cereal are you taking? Is it made from highly purified grain, or does it contain fibre? These small changes over a long period of time can result in big differences in cancer risk. At lunchtime do you have a cooked lunch or just a sandwich? Is it sausages and chips every day, with all the problems of fast food? Or is it a more sensible meal with salad and fruit? In the evening, is it more fast food or a balanced diet? What about snacks between meals, which are often very high in calories? A well-known advertisement for chocolate-coated bars states that it will help you work, rest and play. An occasional bar will do no harm, but eating chocolates regularly, however delicious, can lead to obesity and all its problems. Unfortunately, it is difficult to be dogmatic about dietary advice, but there are some definite pointers which will help you foil cancer.

EATING A HEALTHY DIET

- *Don't worry too much about preservatives in food. On the whole they do more good than harm.*

- *If you are overweight – slim. As well as increasing your risk of certain types of cancer, being fat gives rise to a number of other problems.*

- *Eat less fat – switch from hard cooking fat to oil, avoid fried food and use less butter or switch to low-fat spread, use skimmed milk instead of full-fat milk, use cottage cheese instead of solid cheese.*

- *Eat less sugar – cut down on, or do without, sugar in tea and coffee. Cut down on sweets and snacks – avoid fizzy drinks.*

- *Increase the amount of fibre that you eat. Fibre occurs in bran, cereals, brown bread and fruit.*

- *Make sure you get plenty of vitamins naturally – eat plenty of fruit, don't overcook vegetables (this prevents vitamins from being destroyed, and undercooked vegetables taste better anyway).*

- *The occasional fast-food meal won't do you any harm, but don't let it become a habit!*

ALCOHOL

The association between alcohol and cancer is complex, for it seems to depend on the way in which alcohol is taken as well as on the amount. There may also be multiple factors, including cigarette smoking and diet, involved. In France, large quantities of wine are consumed regularly from an early age. There is good evidence that cancer of the mouth and oesophagus (the tube connecting the mouth to the stomach) are associated with heavy wine consumption. Alcohol, in any form, taken to excess causes serious liver damage. This is through dying liver cells being replaced by defective cells, which in turn leads on to fibrosis of the liver – know also as cirrhosis. Alcoholic cirrhosis causes a high incidence of liver cancer in later life. The type of liver cancer it produces is often widespread and not amenable to most treatments. Small amounts of alcohol are not dangerous, but excess drinking over a period of time will result in an increased cancer incidence. Perhaps more important, of course, are the problems of addiction and the disastrous effects that chronic alcoholism can have on both job and family. There is a slippery slope associated with alcohol intake. Casual drinking can lead to heavy bouts of drinking, and subsequently addictive patterns such as drinking alone or early in the morning.

The recommended safe level of drinking is no more than 21 units a week for men, and no more than 14 units a week for women. This apparent sexual discrimination is because of the different ways in which alcohol is broken down in the two sexes. A unit is equivalent to half-a-pint of beer or cider, or one single measure of spirits, or one glass of wine. Count up how many units you drink in an average week – you may get a nasty shock.

If you think you may be drinking too much, try to cut down. Drink low-alcohol and non-alcoholic drinks instead, and try to go for two or three days without drinking any alcohol at all. In the pub or at a party, space out your alcoholic drinks – have a glass of wine and then a mineral water or a fruit juice. Don't drink regularly to relieve stress, and above all don't feel obliged to drink just because other people are.

Reducing Alcohol Intake

- *Excess alcohol causes 3 per cent of all cancers.*

- *Limit your alcohol intake – less than 21 units per week for men and no more than 14 units per week for women.*

- *Take low-alcohol and non-alcoholic drinks.*

- *Try not to drink every day.*

- *Do not drink regularly to relieve stress.*

- *Do not feel obliged to drink just because other people are.*

- *Seek help if you cannot stop drinking.*

PHYSICAL AGENTS

We are all exposed daily to the physical agents of our environment – such as heat, light, X-rays and gamma rays. Under certain conditions these can cause DNA damage, resulting in growth control abnormalities and subsequently cancer. We will consider each of these physical agents and the measures we can take to reduce their effect on our bodies.

SUNSHINE

Have you ever wondered why the piers dotted around Britain's coasts are so run down? Many are closed, and those that are open are shadows of their former selves. This sad decline reflects a change in holiday pattern for most Britains. The availability of modern jet travel, coupled with the development of cheap tourist trails along the Mediterranean coast, has led many families to take their summer holidays abroad. Even on the hottest summer day, sunshine in Britain is relatively timid compared to that of the Mediterranean. The increasing trend for long-haul holidays to the Caribbean and to other more exotic locations shows that, as leisure time increases, people are more willing to travel further afield in search of the sun.

It has been known for some time that ultraviolet radiation from the sun can cause cancer of the skin, predominantly in the exposed areas of the face and hands, and especially in fair-skinned people. Those who live in hot climates tend to have darker skin. The pigment in the skin absorbs the ultraviolet light, preventing too much damage; thus the skin cancer incidence amongst the Aborigines of Australia is very low, but among the migrants from Europe it is the highest in the world. Although we think of sunbathing as a pleasant and healthy pursuit, the lobster look achieved by so many on their Mediterranean holiday can actually increase the chances of getting certain types of skin cancer at a later date. As well as appearing pretty unpleasant, the lobster look has hidden dangers. The amount of ultraviolet light received by certain cells in the skin can result in serious damage to DNA. This, in turn, can lead to the subsequent development of cancer.

Many skin cancers, if caught early, are easy to treat by surgery or radiotherapy. But, there is one type that can spread and kill – the melanoma. Recent evidence has shown that melanoma incidence has increased rapidly in communities where sun is not a normal feature in their daily life but from which a large number go for sun exposure on their holidays.

The lobster look is easy to avoid. The first step is not to expose large parts of the body immediately – do it slowly. You can get a perfectly reasonable tan over a two-week period without lying on the beach for the whole of the first day. The second step is to use barrier creams which protect the skin from harmful elements of the sun's rays. These creams are now widely available and are very reasonably priced. The use of such creams will considerably reduce your risk of getting sunstroke, and in some cases actually enhance your sun tan. Cheap alcohol in many resorts often results in holidaymakers overindulging at lunchtime and then lying on the beach for the rest of the afternoon. This is extremely dangerous, both in the short term because of sun stroke and in the long term because of the danger of melanoma. Similar problems may arise with certain artificial tanning devices.

REDUCING YOUR RISK

- *Only stay in the sun for a short period to begin with.*

- *Use a sun screen, starting with at least Factor 15 and reducing gradually to Factor 7 as your tan builds up.*

- *Don't be fooled into thinking that just because there is a cool breeze from the sea you aren't likely to get sunburnt. You are. It is just that because the air temperature is cooler you will not notice, until it is too late.*

- *Avoid using sun beds at home. Only use them when super-vised at a health centre. Do not go for a rapid tan, but allow your skin to darken over a period of several weeks. If you are naturally pale, be especially careful to limit exposure to 15 minutes to start with.*

RADIATION

Far more serious, as it remains unseen and in some cases not fully understood, is the effect of radiation. When Wilhelm Konrad Röntgen discovered X-rays 100 years ago in 1895, and Madame Marie Curie isolated radium in the following year, we saw the dawning of the radiation age. It took some four years before the real power of radiation became apparent. Clearly, workers in this area soon developed serious medical problems. Anaemia and a lowering of their white blood cell count was noted, making them susceptible to infections and later to the development of a variety of cancers.

During the First World War large armies of workers sat in huge aircraft hangars painting dials with luminous paint for the control panels of ships and planes. The luminous paint contained small amounts of radium which, over the years, impregnated the workers' skin. To get a fine point on the brush necessary for the intricate work, they would lick the brush, swallowing small amounts of radium salts. They, too, developed anaemia because of failure of their blood-forming cells, and they also developed hideous mouth cancers which were incurable. It is paradoxical that the discovery of radium led to so many cancers as well as providing a cure. Uranium miners in South Africa, who live and work in an atmosphere laden with radon gas, suffer from a much higher incidence of cancer than coalminers. Again, this is because of radioactivity.

The most dramatic episode of the radiation age was the dropping of Trinity – the code name for the first atomic bomb dropped on Hiroshima, followed shortly by another on Nagasaki. At first the true power of the bomb was not realized, although the immediate devastation ended the Second World War and held the world in awe. Out of the rubble of Hiroshima and Nagasaki a more terrible problem emerged. Areas of countryside remained radioactive for long periods of time. Men, women and children rebuilt the cities whilst the background radiation continued to destroy tiny molecular targets in their DNA. The measurement of radiation was very crude in the post-war era. Even so, current estimates suggest that exposure to relatively small amounts of radiation resulted in a much higher incidence of certain cancers. Initially, tumours occurred in the cells of the bone marrow (leukaemias), with the common ones such as those of the lung, breast and colon following.

We are familiar with the evocative photographs of the British and French tests of atom bombs in the early 1950s, with conscripted soldiers lined up against the mushroom cloud of fall-out. Rather like cigarette smoke, it is difficult now to understand why people did not take more precautions. It would be unthinkable today to carry out such tests in the open, and to expose even volunteers to the type of doses these men were receiving.

The 1986 disaster at Chernobyl in the former USSR will give us considerable information about the long-term effects of radiation. The tragedy has been closely monitored, with over 30,000 people undergoing annual checks to compare the dose they received and the subsequent development of various cancers. Already it is clear that the incidence of thyroid cancer is soaring in the southern part of the Ukraine. The reason for this is that radioactive iodine released by the faulty reactor is avidly taken up by the normal thyroid gland, where it is concentrated and, in turn, the radiation causes cancer there. One thing we have learned over the years is that there seems to be no threshold of safe radiation. This means that we must strive for the minimum possible exposure in the workplace and in the environment. But the risks are all relative. Getting down to zero radiation would be impossible because of the natural components in the environment.

But we can try to avoid unnecessary radiation. We use X-rays for diagnosis and therapy. We produce electricity in nuclear power stations and we use atomic bombs for political reasons to hold the balance of power between various countries. In addition, we are in a universe where radiation is very much part of life. What can we do to minimize our exposure?

The evidence that people living next door to a nuclear power plant or hospital radiation therapy department have a higher risk of developing cancer is just not there. Many surveys have been carried out, resulting in confusing statistics. A good example is the demonstration of a small increase in cancer risk in children living in West Cumbria near the Sellafield Nuclear Processing Plant. Subsequent studies suggest that the increased incidence of leukaemia found there is not because of radiation but from other factors related to the age distribution of the population who moved there to work in and around the plant. But we must all play our part campaigning to keep our environment safe.

There are some types of radiation we can do very little about. For example, cosmic rays from the sun and emissions of radon from certain building materials. Thanks to the setting up of rigorous safety procedures, there is little risk of cancer from radiation used in the workplace. People working in X-ray departments and factories where X-rays are used no longer have a higher incidence of cancer.

The casual use of X-rays for shoe fitting has long since stopped, but still too many X-rays are done unnecessarily in our hospitals. You have a personal responsibility for your health and if an X-ray is requested by your doctor you are quite entitled to ask how it will help in your diagnosis and treatment. One of the big bugbears of medicine is the frequent repetition of blood tests and X-rays by junior doctors to avoid any criticism that they have left out important tests. If you are sent from one hospital to another for investigations it is all too easy just to repeat a whole set of X-rays rather than to obtain the old ones, which are unlikely to change over a short period of time.

A major dilemma has crept in with mammography in breast cancer screening. Mammograms (X-rays of the breast) are a very good way of telling whether a patient has a small lump that may be malignant. Mammographic screening has been introduced in the UK, but there are many opponents to it. The number of lives saved by mammographic screening is low compared with the cost both in financial and hassle terms when, indeed, it is only in the 50–64 year-old age group that any survival benefit has been found from screening. Opponents of the introduction of the screening programme suggest that the X-rays used for the mammograms will in fact increase the risk of breast cancer. Unfortunately, we have no solid information either way. The individual X-ray dose accumulated over a large number of years may well be significant. There appears to be no lower threshold for cancer induction by radiation. This means that even trivial amounts of radiation may be important. Unborn babies and children are more susceptible as their tissues are more easily damaged, and perhaps their repair processes are not as effective. It has been shown that women who have had X-rays during pregnancy have a higher risk of producing abnormal babies. The most sensitive period is the first three months. Therefore, if you think you may be pregnant, tell your doctor before he sends you off for X-rays. Some X-ray investigations involve a much bigger dose of radiation than others. X-rays that are performed at the dentist, for example, use almost trivial amounts of radiation, whereas those to examine the kidneys require a large amount. The best advice if you are pregnant is to keep asking the doctors and radiographers about the need for the investigation and whether it can be delayed until the pregnancy is completed. Certain types of investigation can even cause young children who are being breast-fed to become radioactive.

REDUCING RADIATION EXPOSURE

- *Avoid unnecessary X-ray examinations – this is particularly important with pregnant women.*

- *Observe safety regulations at work.*

- *Campaign for a safer environment.*

BIOLOGICAL FACTORS IN CANCER

Is cancer infectious? This is another common question in the clinic. The answer to nearly every patient is no. But there are cancers in animals which are caused by viruses, and there are some human tumours which are either directly caused by or related to viral infection.

Viruses

In 1910 Francis Peyton Rous, working in a laboratory in New York City, was puzzled by an observation he made. A farmer friend told him that some of his chickens developed curious sarcomas, tumours under the skin, around the thigh. He did an experiment which showed that cell-free extract of the tumour could actually cause new cancers in other chickens. He discovered the virus that bears his name – Rous' sarcoma virus. There are many similar viruses which cause cancer in hamsters, rats, mice, cats and even chimpanzees.

By 1970 a lot of information had been gathered about these viruses, yet none had been found directly to infect humans. Then a very puzzling observation was made. Along the coast of southern Japan there are many fishing communities. The communities are very close-knit, as access to many of the villages is difficult, some being accessible only by boat. In the local hospital a physician noted that many villagers were getting a curious tumour of the lymph glands called T-cell lymphoma. Sometimes they had a form of leukaemia: instead of the lymph nodes being enlarged the abnormal cells from the lymph nodes burst out into the circulation and could be seen in the blood under the microscope. T-cell lymphoma was incredibly rare in most parts of the world but relatively common in fishing villages in southern Japan. Blood from these patients was collected and found to contain a virus similar to Rous' sarcoma virus. Subsequently, a virus was isolated and material collected from one of the patients. The virus was called human T-cell lymphoma virus I, or HTLVI. Although a very rare cause of human cancer, the virus was to become enshrined in the history of medicine. It subsequently led to the discovery of its close relative HTLVIII, now called HIV, the human immunodeficiency virus and the cause of AIDS. The viruses are very similar in structure, though HTLVI is not spread by the same routes. So far it is the only virus of its type that has been directly associated with human cancer.

HIV, the virus which causes AIDS, has now become the most prominent of the viruses which is transmitted by sex. Although AIDS patients develop cancer (often a very rare type of skin tumour called Kaposi's sarcoma), the reason the disease is so lethal is that the immune system is essentially wiped out. This leads to infections going out of control, especially of the lungs. The virus probably does not cause the cancer directly but rather by removing the immune system's ability to deal with wayward cells when they arise.

It has been known for some time that amongst communities where promiscuity is low, there is a low incidence of cervical cancer. Furthermore, such tumours often contain small viruses related to those that cause genital warts – the human papilloma virus. Recent observations implicated a specific type of papilloma virus – type 16 – in the majority of cancers of the cervix. Clearly, it is not the only cause of the disease. It appears to be part of the natural history.

Denis Burkitt, a British surgeon working in Uganda, was

curious about a very unusual lymphoma, which now bears his name, that he noted in children in various parts of Africa, such as Uganda – usually in the areas in which malaria was rife. Although often presenting itself in an advanced stage, with horrible lesions around the mouth and the back of the eye, the disease could often be treated by very simple chemotherapy. In the late 1960s a virus was discovered growing out of Burkitt's lymphoma tissue. This was called the Epstein-Barr virus. Quite by chance, Epstein-Barr virus was also found to be the cause of glandular fever, a very common illness in Britain. Glandular fever is not a cancer, although lymphocytes are stimulated to cause swelling in the throat and in the neck lymph nodes. Burkitt's lymphoma, however, is lethal unless treated. But there is a paradox. Glandular fever is common in this country and in America, and yet the incidence of Burkitt's lymphoma is extremely low. Even to this day the paradox has not been resolved.

The most likely scenario is that the Epstein-Barr virus is just one of the several factors which leads to Burkitt's lymphoma. Chronic malaria infection in the areas of the world where Burkitt's lymphoma is found can stimulate the immune system. The number of white blood cells increases dramatically, so that there are many more target cells for the Epstein-Barr virus to hit. Although the immune system is stimulated by the paramalaria parasite, it may well not be so effective at controlling the regeneration of abnormal cells. This may make lymphocytes ineffective and allow the Epstein-Barr virus to grow in a more uncontrolled way, leading to the lymphoma.

Another common viral disease in the Third World that is definitely associated with a specific cancer type is hepatitis B. This can be spread by a variety of routes – eating infected shellfish, transfusion of contaminated blood, sexual intercourse and, on some occasions, by direct contact. It causes inflammation of the liver, hence the name hepatitis. Although the lives of some patients may be threatened by declining liver function, with jaundice, most patients make a full recovery. About 5 per cent of patients in those countries where malnutrition is rife go on to develop chronic hepatitis after many years. It is under these conditions that cancer of the liver (hepatoma) seems to arise. The hepatitis virus is incorporated into the malignant cells, suggesting that it may play a part in causing the cancer. It may well be disrupting those genes responsible for normal growth control, as well as stimulating the abnormal growth cells in certain areas of the liver.

In the vast majority of cancers there is no evidence to suggest that viruses are responsible. Generally speaking, cancer is not 'catching'. Where viruses have been implicated in the development of cancer (e.g. lymphoma and hepatoma following hepatitis) other factors, such as malaria or malnutrition, have played an important part.

The exception to this is cancers arising from sexually transmitted viruses. There are several links between sex and cancer. Nuns, for example, have a very low incidence of cervical cancer. Almost certainly, the lack of sexual partners reduces the risk of infection by viruses or other agents that over a long period of time may cause changes in the lining in the neck of the womb. That is not to say, of course, that women who have many sexual partners will necessarily get cervical cancer, but just that the probability is increased. Prostitutes, who over many years will have had multiple partners, are at greatest risk, not only from AIDS but also from cervical cancer. There is increasing evidence associating the disease with various wart viruses, although the relationship is complex. The best advice is to try to keep the number of sexual contacts to a minimum, and to use barrier contraceptives, such as a condom, which protect against direct contact with viruses.

The same advice applies to avoiding AIDS. Casual sex without condom usage is fraught with hazards and should be avoided. The most dangerous scenario is in holiday areas where prostitutes may well have bisexual men on their list of customers. In some underdeveloped areas, screening for viral infection may not be possible and the risk is increased. The best advice one can give is to avoid casual sex completely.

Cancer of the penis is relatively rare now. It usually occurs in elderly men and is often associated with poor hygiene. It is declining rapidly because of the increased awareness of the importance of hygiene generally, and obviously the increased facilities for washing. There is some evidence for linkage of this tumour with cancer of the cervix, in that the same virus types appear to be involved in triggering both diseases. Attention to personal hygiene and using a condom during casual sex are probably the two best measures to try to reduce further the already low incidence.

REDUCING RISK FROM BIOLOGICAL FACTORS

- *When visiting certain countries vaccination against hepatitis is recommended. Ask your doctor for details.*

- *Avoid casual sex where possible.*

- *Always use a condom to reduce the risk of infection.*

- *Keep the number of sexual contacts to a minimum.*

- *See your doctor if you have any persistent discharge or discomfort.*

- *Women who are, or have been, sexually active should screen for cervical cancer every three years. This should include an examination and a cervical smear.*

HORMONES AND CANCER

Hormones are the chemical controllers of the body. They are released by glandular structures of the body as signals to other organs to implement change. There are many different hormones, some of which have a very profound influence on the way in which cells grow in different tissues. Sex hormones, for example, control the growth and development of breasts and uterus in women, and testes in men. The cyclical release of the appropriate sex hormones in women results in the menstrual cycle, the shedding of the lining of the womb at monthly intervals. Individuals have their own hormonal make up. For many years it has been realized that certain hormonal patterns may be associated with a higher or lower incidence of cancer, most usually of the breast or uterus. The age of a woman when she had her first period, the number of pregnancies, her age at the time, whether or not she breast-fed her children and the age at which she reached the menopause all affect hormonal levels on the normal breast, and thus the likelihood of cancer in this area.

There is considerable controversy as to the cancer risk involved in manipulating the hormonal systems of the body. Hormonal manipulation has been used for many years either for birth control (the contraceptive pill) or to prevent bone destruction after the menopause in women (hormone replacement therapy). Certain types of contraceptive pill containing a high level of oestrogen have been associated with a higher than normal incidence of cancer in the breast and uterus, whilst those with a low dose may well have a protective effect.

It is clear that subtle changes in our hormonal make up can cause long-term and unfavourable changes in various structures. As we learn more about the various factors that control growth in many tissues, we may become aware of how manipulations in the hormonal system can affect these and change the pattern of cancer incidence.

REDUCING HORMONAL RISK

- *If you are taking oral contraceptives, make sure they are of the low oestrogen type. If you are not sure, see your doctor.*

- *If you have taken the pill for many years, consider alternative forms of contraception.*

- *If your doctor recommends hormone replacement therapy after the menopause, make sure you try to stop it once the symptoms disappear, and certainly after two–three years.*

- *Take part in the various screening programmes offered for breast and gynaecological cancers. Again, your doctor has the details.*

YOUR HEALTH IS YOUR BUSINESS

Any of our recommendations in this book will reduce your chances of several diseases, and therefore allow you to live longer. These include problems with the heart and lungs, gallstones, kidney stones and the many unpleasant ailments related to behaviour patterns of modern society. There has to be an element of single-mindedness about your approach. There is no way a heavy smoker will succeed in giving up smoking without endless willpower and drive. Similarly, if you are overweight, it is difficult to slim rapidly and not regain weight, but it is by no means impossible.

Taking a reasonable amount of exercise is vital. The evidence that lack of exercise is directly related to the risk of getting cancer is small. However, exercise is part of a healthy lifestyle that will reduce the risks of cancer. There is no need to get carried away. Many joggers ostentatiously running round in the latest jogging gear may be hammering their bodies in a most dangerous way. Walking to work, using the stairs instead of the lift, going for a walk instead of lying on the beach all day on holiday, these are all ways of increasing exercise in moderation. They will all help you avoid the sedentary lifestyle which many of us now live.

There are some very easy examinations which you can and should carry out regularly on yourself as a means of detecting symptoms early. For breast cancer in women and testicular cancer in men, details will be found in subsequent pages.

There are a few diseases for which screening programmes can be effective. The one that is clear-cut is cancer of the cervix. Here, we screen not only for cancer itself but for a pre-malignant state in the lining in the neck of the uterus. Breast cancer screening is more controversial. Some people feel every woman should be screened from the age of 35 onwards, whilst others believe that the screening programme X-rays could actually result in an increased cancer risk. The whole area is shrouded with politics. No government wants to be seen standing in the way of promoting better health, but the cost of screening is enormous and the resources could well be spent more productively in other areas to improve the health of the nation.

The best place for co-ordinating health screening is the general practitioner's surgery. We are very privileged in Britain to have such an excellent system of primary care. The GP is the best person to provide advice about screening and, in fact, they can organize most of it.

If after reading this you feel that there are aspects of your lifestyle that could be improved, but you are not sure how to go about it, then consult your GP. If you are a heavy smoker, your doctor may put you in touch with local anti-smoking groups. If you are overweight, he or she will help by suggesting various diets, and also by checking other diseases associated with obesity, such as high blood pressure. Use your GP as a counsellor. Any doctor would rather take your blood pressure today than see you in a year's time in the middle of the night after you have had a stroke.

CANCER SCREENING

We know that people who have small tumours are less likely to have metastases, and so respond better to treatment. It would, therefore, seem logical that detecting tumours early would give better results. Unfortunately, this does not always follow. Some very small tumours can be extremely aggressive, spreading widely before they can be detected by any known test. Furthermore, for every person found to have cancer, many more will have suspicious abnormalities on the screening test that will require further investigation. This greatly adds to the cost of screening and, of course, to the level of anxiety of those taking part.

Cervical Cancer

By taking a small sample of cells from the cervix using a wooden spatula and smearing these cells on to a glass slide, changes in pattern can be detected which may suggest the subsequent development of cancer. This allows appropriate and very simple treatment to take place long before a tumour appears. For this reason cervical smears are a very effective screening method. Current recommendations suggest that they should be done every three years from the age of 25–40. They are performed by GPs, gynaecology, antenatal and family planning clinics. There is little controversy about their effectiveness.

Breast Cancer

In 1989 the Department of Health launched a national breast cancer screening programme. This was based on data from large studies in New York and Stockholm and a pilot study in Britain of the use of special X-rays for the breast (mammogram) and clinical examination in large groups of women. This whole area is filled with controversy. Let us explain.

Although the New York data clearly showed an advantage for screening, the Stockholm data are not so clear. In the studies, the specialists involved in reading X-rays and performing the clinical examinations became very experienced and adept at picking up on abnormalities that may be missed when the techniques are adapted for the fast turnover necessary for community screening. Furthermore, although the lesions picked up on screening are small, it does not necessarily mean that such patients will actually do better. If the disease has already spread when the diagnosis is made, early detection is not necessarily of value. It could be that rapidly growing and spreading tumours may be picked up more readily by screening. A further problem is how often to do the mammograms. The current recommendation is every three years. Mammograms involve the use of X-rays which may themselves induce cancer. So, unlike cervical screening, there is a definite risk of harm with regular mammography.

A simpler and cheaper way of screening is for women to be aware of any changes in their breasts. Although the value of regular self-examination has been questioned in recent years, it is felt worth while for women to be 'aware' of their breasts. For those between the ages of 50 and 64 there does seem to be definite benefit in three-yearly mammography. Under 50 there is no such benefit demonstrated as yet, and we do not recommend it. See Figure 2.3 for a diagram showing you the principles of breast awareness.

Health care and politics really do not mix. For political reasons the Government in the late 1980s introduced the national breast screening programme. This created a lot of anxiety, and it might have been better to wait until more data became available. The one good thing it has produced is the streamlined service for people with breast abnormalities. Non-stop clinics, where a woman can have a biopsy, counselling and the result as quickly as possible, can certainly reduce the anxiety level in women with a problem.

It is possible the breast screening programme will change when good genetic tests for breast cancer come into operation. These are likely over the next five years and will identify a group of women who have a very high risk of developing breast cancer. It may well be worth screening these women at a much earlier age and with more intensive techniques. It may also allow the majority of the population to avoid unnecessary screening.

What is Breast Awareness?

Breast awareness is the process of getting to know your breasts and finding what is normal for you. When you know how your breasts normally look and feel, you will be the first to notice any changes.

Most changes are harmless but should be checked by a doctor. These are seldom cancer but, if it is, early detection means simpler and usually more successful treatment.

When Should I Check?

This is up to you, but you have probably noticed that your breasts change during your monthly cycle.

Many women have lumpy and tender breasts just before their period.

After the menopause normal breasts feel soft and less lumpy.

What Should I Check For?

Remember you are looking for *any* change in your breasts which is unusual *for you.*

Figure 2.3 *Breast awareness.*

1) Stand with your arms hanging loosely by your sides and look at your breasts in the mirror. Go through this checklist.

Is there:

any change in the size, shape or colour of your breasts?
any change in the nipples?
any bleeding or discharge from the nipples?
any unusual puckering or dimpling on the breast or nipple?
any vein standing out in a way that's not usual for you?

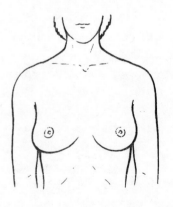

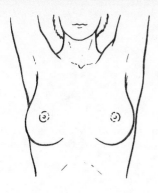

2) *Now raise your arms above your head. Turn from side to side to see your breasts from different angles.*

Go through the checklist again.

Put your hands on your hips and press.

Go through the checklist again.

3) *Lie down on your bed with your head on a pillow. Put a folded towel under the shoulder blade of the side you are examining – this helps to flatten the breast tissue and makes it easier to examine.*

Use your left hand to examine your right breast and vice versa. Put the hand you're not using on the pillow under your head.

As you examine your breast, keep the fingers of the hand together. Use the flat of the fingers, not the tips.

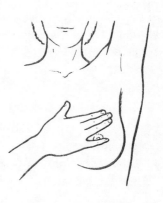

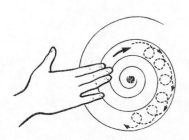

4) *Trace a continuous spiral around the breast, moving your fingers in small circles and using firm pressure. Start by feeling around the nipple and then work outwards until you have felt every part of your breast. A ridge of firm tissue in a half-moon shape under the breast is quite normal: this helps to support your breast.*

5) *Bring the arm resting on the pillow down by your side. Using your left hand to examine the right-hand side of your body, feel the part of your breast that goes up as far as the collarbone. Then feel the part that goes into the armpit, and work your way back towards your breast.*

Now change sides and examine the other breast in exactly the same way with your other hand.

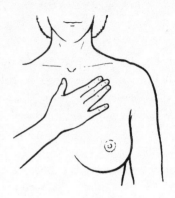

If you do find something unusual in one breast, always check the other breast for the same thing – it may just be the way your breasts are made.

Colon Cancer

Although colon cancer is common, it often takes time for gastrointestinal symptoms, such as diarrhoea, abdominal pain and so on, to become apparent, by which time the disease is established and may well have spread. Such tumours eventually break through the lining of the colon and are directly exposed to the contents of the bowel. Here they may bleed, producing a tiny trickle of blood. This goes unnoticed until a moderately enlarged blood vessel is eroded. There are chemical tests available to detect even traces of blood in the stool. An innovative approach is to coat toilet paper with a detector for small amounts of blood. If this changes colour the patient is asked to go to see their doctor. The problem is that many people have small amounts of blood in their stool caused by piles and other quite benign problems. Therefore, a large number of people come forward who are found subsequently not to have cancer.

In the United States the American Cancer Society is much more aggressive in its recommendations for screening for colo-rectal cancer. It recommends annual check-ups, including examination of the lower part of the colon, for everyone over the age of 55. The evidence that this reduces mortality from colo-rectal cancer still remains to be seen. Another development in this country has been the use of the flexible fibre optic sigmoidoscope, a flexible tube that can be inserted into the colon painlessly. By detecting polyps, which are benign lesions, by a single screening at the age of 50, it has been calculated that a large number of colon cancers will be prevented. A large study is about to start in Britain to test this hypothesis.

Lung Cancer

Until 1970, tuberculosis was fairly widespread in the UK. Chest X-rays were performed regularly to look for the disease. TB is now readily treatable, but lung cancer has been increasing. Despite several studies with repeated chest X-rays to screen for lung cancer, no benefit has been found, and although new patients are picked up by screening there is no evidence that they respond better to existing therapy than those picked up when symptoms develop. For this reason, regular chest X-rays, even in heavy smokers to pick up lung cancer, are no longer performed.

Testicular Cancer

Although relatively rare, this type of cancer is easily treatable. It occurs mainly in young men. Regular self-examination (*see Figure 2.4*) will enable it to be detected at an early stage. See your doctor if you think there is an abnormality.

Figure 2.4 *Testicular self-examination.*

1) *You should examine your testicles regularly – say, once a month. It's easier to do this after a warm bath or shower, when the scrotal skin is relaxed. If you do notice anything unusual, make an appointment to see your doctor straight away. It won't necessarily be cancer, but it's best to put your mind at rest.*

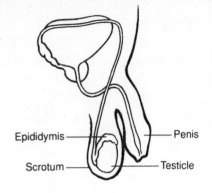

Epididymis — | — Penis

Scrotum — | — Testicle

2) *Hold your scrotum in the palms of your hands. This allows you to use the thumb and fingers of both hands to examine your testicles.*

Note their size and weight. It's normal for one testicle to be larger than the other, but they should be roughly the same weight.

3) *Feel each testicle individually. You should be able to feel a soft tube at the top and back of the testicle. This is the epididymis, which carries and stores sperm and should not be confused with an abnormal lump.*

Check each testicle for any lumps, swellings, slight enlargement or change in firmness. Normally, testicles should be smooth without any lumps.

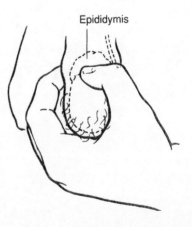

Epididymis

There are several other experimental screening programmes for different tumour types. Rather than worry about whether to take part, the best advice is to take a high level of personal responsibility for your own health care. If you are worried about cancer, go to see your GP – the best person to advise about screening.

CANCER CHECKLIST

- *A lump anywhere in the body.*

- *A change in a skin mole.*

- *Any unusual bleeding in urine or stool, or in any discharge.*

- *Persistent diarrhoea or constipation.*

- *Persistent cough or hoarseness.*

- *Unexplained weight loss.*

- *If you experience any of these, consult your doctor.*

CONCLUSION

The probability of getting cancer is high, with the disease affecting one in four of us, but we can tip the odds in our favour by adopting a sensible lifestyle. In doing so, our level of health generally will improve, and the chance of living to old age increases. Although there will be improvements over the next two decades, some of the most common cancers are likely to remain difficult to treat until well into the next century. More effort spent on prevention could pay big dividends.

ARE YOU AT RISK?

One in three of us will get cancer. We have outlined some of the
ways we can avoid it. How does your lifestyle measure up?
Complete the following questions and add up your marks.

SCORE

Do you smoke? ...

nothing	0
fewer than 10 cigarettes a day	5
10–20 cigarettes a day	20
more than 20 cigarettes a day	30

Five years ago did you smoke? ...

nothing	0
fewer than 10 cigarettes a day	3
10–20 cigarettes a day	12
more than 20 cigarettes a day	16
an occasional cigar/pipe	4

**Is there a heavy smoker in your house or the room in which
you work?**

yes	2
no	0

Take your height in metres and multiply it by itself.
Take your weight in kilograms and divide it by this number.
Is your score? ...

MEN	WOMEN	
20–25	*19–24*	0
26–27	*25–26*	6
more than 27	*more than 26*	10

Do you eat fast food, e.g. hamburgers, hot dogs, fish and chips? ...

more than once weekly	2
less than once weekly	1
rarely	0

Do you eat meat? ...

twice daily	2
once daily	1
occasionally/never	0

Do you eat high-fibre cereal for breakfast? ...

every day	0
three times weekly	1
rarely	3

You are being taken out for dinner in your favourite restaurant. Which of the following items on the menu would you prefer? ...

vegetable soup	0
prawn cocktail	1
brown bread	0
white bread	1
avocado vinaigrette	0
deep-fried mushrooms	1
chicken salad	0
steak and chips	1
gooseberry pie and cream	1
fresh fruit salad	0
Black Forest gâteau	2
cream caramel	0

Do you go abroad for holidays to a warmer climate?

yes   1

no   0

Do you use a barrier sun cream at least at the start of the holiday?

yes   0

no   1

Does your skin go bright red for several days before a tan develops?

yes   3

no   1

Does your job involve strenuous physical labour?

yes   3

no   1

Do you exercise or perform a physical sport at least once a week?

yes   0

no   2

Do you walk at least one mile on an average day?

yes   1

no   2

If you are a woman, do you take a contraceptive pill?

yes   1

no   0

How many sexual partners have you had?

1–5   0

5–10   2

more than 10   3

If you have sexual relationships, do you use a barrier contraceptive method, e.g. condom or cap?

yes	0
no	1

How many first degree relatives (i.e. father, mother, brother, sister) have had cancer?

none	0
1	1
2	2
more than 2	5

How much alcohol do you drink per week? (one unit is a single measure of gin, whisky, etc., or half-a-pint of beer, lager or cider)

none	0
1–14 units	2
14–30 units	4
more than 30 units	6

TOTAL

Well, how did you get on? If you have been honest, your score will provide a cancer probability rating relative to your current lifestyle. For most things, including smoking, it is not too late to change.

SCORING

80–100   A very high cancer risk. You smoke heavily and are
          likely to be overweight. It's not just cancer that will
          kill you. Now is the time to change. See your doctor
          soon.

60-80   You have a high chance of getting cancer. You must
          cut down on smoking. Look at the rest of your
          lifestyle.

40–60   Watch it. Take the advice offered and review how you
          live.

20–40   Not bad. But be careful and follow the advice.

0–20   Low cancer risk. Keep going. There's no guarantee
          you won't get the disease, but you're doing all you
          can to avoid it.

CHAPTER THREE

Diagnosing Cancer?

J ust as no two individuals are alike, no two cancers are exactly the same. There are many symptoms which might indicate cancer, and different symptoms cause different degrees of alarm in patients and their families. For example, the coughing up of a small amount of blood, annoying chest pain, or persistent profound diarrhoea, rapidly send patients to their doctor. However, a slight shortness of breath, a general feeling of fatigue and loss of appetite may be ascribed to some temporary illness and be shrugged off. How is the diagnosis of cancer made?

As we have explained, cancer is a disease of cells. The only way to diagnose cancer conclusively is to test a small sample of the abnormal cells. The usual way of doing this is to obtain a biopsy. All this means is that a small piece of tissue is examined by one method or another. Before a biopsy is performed, the doctor will ask a series of questions to try to find out the cause of the symptoms. There is no specific symptom of cancer: it depends on where the tumour is, how big it is, which structures it is invading and whether it has spread to other parts of the body. A patient with lung cancer, for example, may have a cough (sometimes with blood or phlegm) or a persistent chest infection which does not respond to antibiotics. Non-specific symptoms, such as fatigue, weight loss, loss of appetite and depression, can also occur. The usual symptom of breast cancer is a lump in the breast, although it may well spread before it can be detected in this way. If it does so, the symptoms it produces will depend on the site to which it spreads. If it spreads to the lungs then it may mimic a lung tumour; if it goes to the liver, a liver tumour ... and so forth. Cancer of the cervix can cause abnormal bleeding between periods or persistent bleeding in women who have already reached the menopause; patients suffering from colon cancer may have abdominal pain, diarrhoea or blood in the stools. Every symptom that cancer produces can be mimicked by completely benign and harmless conditions. Just as a chest infection can mimic lung cancer, most lumps in the breast are not because of cancer. If the symptoms cannot be controlled by straightforward temporary medication of the sort usually available in every household, then you should consult your GP, who will decide what further tests are necessary.

The first thing a doctor will do is examine you, noting your pulse, temperature and sometimes blood pressure. They will examine your chest and abdomen, listening for abnormal function of the lungs, and feeling for abnormal masses in the liver, spleen and other abdominal organs. Blood tests to see if you are anaemic or have a low white blood cell count, and tests for kidney and liver function, may also be carried out. A chest X-ray and more specific tests may be requested depending on the likely site of the primary tumour. There is a whole range of investigations which can be performed. At this stage the GP or family doctor may already have a good idea of what is wrong, and will refer you to a surgeon at a hospital so that the biopsy can be performed. In some countries you may not go through a family practitioner, but will be seen directly by a surgeon because of the nature of your symptoms. This is most likely in North America. If cancer is diagnosed, you will usually see a specialist for further treatment.

Sometimes the diagnosis can be made without a biopsy. A diagnosis of lung cancer can be made by seeing abnormal cells in the sputum which is coughed into a container and examined under the microscope. Similarly, if fluid has gathered in the cavity surrounding the intestines, then simply putting a needle in — a relatively painless process — and removing a few drops of fluid can provide a diagnosis. In most cases, however, the surgeon will obtain a biopsy under anaesthetic.

DIAGNOSING CANCER

- *Blood tests can check for anaemia, bone marrow function, how the liver and kidneys are working.*

- *Some cancers secrete substances which can be detected in the blood.*

- *Plain X-rays provide information about various parts of the body.*

- *Contrast X-rays, performed by giving an injection or drink of a substance which will show up on the X-ray, can be more useful.*

- *CT (computerized tomography) scans or MRI (magnetic resonance imager) scans may provide detailed information about the structure of vital organs.*

- *Bone and liver scans can show areas of defective function which may be caused by a tumour.*

- *A biopsy – the sampling of a piece of tissue thought to contain the cancer – is the definitive way to make the diagnosis.*

BIOPSY

Usually, the only certain way to make a diagnosis of cancer is to take a biopsy of the affected part of the body. This is just a sample of living tissue. If the tumour is very small it may be completely removed and the whole sample sent to the laboratory for examination. If it is larger, then a tiny fragment may be taken.

It is obviously easy to obtain a sample of tissue from the surface, so samples of skin tumours can be taken under local anaesthetic. This is done in the clinic and takes only a few minutes. An antiseptic solution is wiped over the area to be sampled and, using a very fine needle, local anaesthetic is injected. There is a tiny prick to start with and then the area becomes numb in about 20 seconds. A doctor makes a small nick in the skin with a scalpel and cuts out a small sample. A single stitch may be all that is needed to allow healing. After a few days the wound heals completely, leaving a small scar which, in turn, will disappear.

Tumours which lie under the skin are more difficult to get at. A swollen lymph gland in the neck, for example, may move around making biopsy under local anaesthetic uncomfortable and difficult. In these circumstances the patient is given a general anaesthetic and has a small operation carried out in the operating theatre. The procedure is painless. By doing this the muscles of the body relax, allowing the doctor to obtain a much better impression of where the tumour really is. Indeed, examination under anaesthetic, or EUA for short, is sometimes an essential part of defining how far a tumour has spread. This is particularly true in the pelvis, where it is difficult to examine patients without discomfort whilst they are awake.

If the tumour is deep inside a hollow organ of the body, then an endoscope is used. Endoscopy (looking inside the body) involves passing a fine, flexible tube, made of optical fibres, through the body's natural openings to reach the site to be examined. A small sample of tissue is then removed. Common sites where endoscopy is performed include the oesophagus, stomach, rectum, colon, lungs and peritoneal cavity of the abdomen. Nowadays, this can be performed under local anaesthetic and is surprisingly painless.

Take endoscopy of the stomach, for example. There is no need to stay in hospital overnight, unless you live a long way away, or other tests are going to be done at the same time. You will be asked not to eat anything for several hours beforehand so that your stomach is empty, to give the doctor a better view. A sedative injection is given and a tube is placed in your mouth and gradually swallowed. When it reaches your stomach, the doctor can look down the eyepiece for a perfect view of the inside stomach wall. There is a camera attachment so that a full record can be made, enabling the images to be seen in colour on a monitor, which is useful for training purposes. You will not be able to see the monitor yourself as you are being endoscoped, but if you are interested, ask to see the photographs afterwards. A biopsy of any suspicious area can be taken, using an attached remote-controlled fine pair of tweezers. As there are no nerve fibres inside the stomach there is no pain at all when the tweezers are used. This applies to all areas which are endoscoped. The tube is then removed, and after a short rest you can go home. The actual procedure only takes a few minutes.

Increasingly, needle biopsies are performed on many parts of the body. Like endoscopy, the whole business is almost painless. Local anaesthetic is used to numb the sensitive nerve fibres lying under the skin. A fine needle 2–10 cm long is then passed through the skin into the area thought to contain a tumour. The needle is connected to a syringe that sucks up a few cells from this area. The needle is then withdrawn and the cells are pushed out on to a glass slide for examination under a microscope. The whole procedure takes only a few minutes. Sometimes this may be done under X-ray control to ensure that the needle is in exactly the right place – for example, when sampling an unusual shadow on a chest X-ray to see if it is lung cancer. In many instances the local anaesthetic may not be necessary, and this is particularly true when fine needle samples are taken from breast lumps. Having a local anaesthetic requires two needles to be inserted, whereas if the sample is simply taken with one needle it is actually less painful.

The tissue sample – whether taken by open biopsy, endoscopy or using a fine needle – is then sent to the pathology laboratory to be examined. The tissue is embedded in wax, if it is sufficiently large, or looked at directly on a slide in the case of a fine needle sample. Sections of large biopsies are then cut using a sharp knife. These are layered on to a microscope slide, stained with dyes which will outline the shapes of the cells and their nuclei, and reviewed by the pathologists. Their job is to assess exactly what is going on in the tissue. The pathologist's skills are absolutely vital in sorting out whether a particular abnormality is benign or malignant. This is done by recognizing patterns in the tissue. With experience, the pathologist can quickly define the nature of the lesion. This is essential in deciding on the best treatment.

X-RAY INVESTIGATIONS

X-rays are often used as quick diagnostic tests, either before or after the biopsy. The most common X-ray is that of the chest. This provides information about the size of the heart, the presence of tumours in the lungs or in the lymph nodes at the centre of the chest, and also whether any of the bone structure of the ribs and spine has been infiltrated by tumour. X-rays yield information because they penetrate tissues differently, producing images of bone, lungs, fat and so forth. But, while they are very good for detecting broken bones, they are not so good for looking at subtle changes in the soft tissues of the body. A 2 cm lung tumour is visible on a chest X-ray, but a 2 cm colon tumour could not be seen on an abdominal X-ray. There is little difference in the water content of a tumour in the abdomen and the surrounding tissue. Newer X-ray technology has been developed to overcome this problem.

Over the last 10 to 15 years computerized tomographic (CT) scans have become widespread. CT scanners are often known as cancer scanners, although they have many more uses than simply detecting cancer. When having a scan, the patient lies on a table for about half-an-hour while a huge revolving disc moves up and down, taking X-rays. A computer then calculates the tissue density at many defined sites in the body. In this way, the scanner produces a series of slices outlining internal structures based on their different water content. The whole procedure is completely painless. CT scans are very useful in measuring the size of the tumour and assessing how far a tumour has spread, particularly in the abdomen. In the past decade the technology has improved dramatically and we are now able to see clearly much smaller changes and abnormalities than was once the case. In addition to CT scanning, magnetic resonance imaging (MRI) has also become increasingly widespread. This involves the patient lying within a large, long tube. It is a rather more claustrophobic investigation than a CT scan! Essentially, the patient is placed within a large magnetic field, and changes within this magnetic field are then analysed. In some areas, for example the brain and the pelvis, which are surrounded by bone, images produced by MRI are of better quality than CT. Abnormalities which are not evident on CT scans may be evident on MRI scans. As MRI scans become more widely available the technique is being used increasingly, but as the equipment is significantly more expensive than CT scanners it is likely that you may have to travel for this examination to be performed.

X-ray examinations can also be performed using contrast fluid. This allows the structure of various internal organs to be seen more clearly. The most common contrast is the barium meal or swallow. This involves your being given a chalky white fluid, containing barium sulphate, to drink after fasting for four hours. Your stomach should be empty after the fast, so the barium flows freely around the inner lining. The barium can be seen on an X-ray screen, and pictures are taken of any suspicious areas. Whilst not exactly champagne, the fluid does not taste too bad, despite all the rumours. The doctor performing the investigation may put you in unusual positions so that the barium can swirl around in the stomach to provide the best pictures and show up any irregularities. Sometimes the X-rays are good enough to determine diagnosis, but often a biopsy is needed to confirm it.

Ultrasound is a completely painless procedure in which sound waves are sent into the body and their echoes recorded and used to build up an image of the body cavities. For this procedure, some jelly is rubbed on the skin and a metal probe placed over the relevant areas. Tumours in the abdomen and pelvis can often be identified and their growth pattern followed using this method. It is also used in pregnancy to monitor growth of the foetus – so it is very safe. In addition, it is cheaper and more widely available than CT or MRI scanning, and consequently may be used to follow up abdominal tumours, such as ovarian cancers, once the initial diagnosis and primary treatment have been completed.

So, it is not essential to have complex and expensive investigations. This is not meanness on the part of the doctors responsible for your management. Diagnostic tests are only undertaken if they are going to help in the choice of treatment by providing valuable information on the size of the tumour and how far it has spread.

2

Treatment

CHAPTER FOUR

The System
and How It Functions

Wherever we may live in the world, it is usually from expert medical diagnosis that we learn whether suspected symptoms are actually cancer. The initial diagnosis will probably have arisen from a biopsy. In most cases, this will be confirmed by a surgeon, and you may also be seen by a physician who carries out investigations which lead to the diagnosis of cancer. These two doctors, although specialists, are not usually specialists in the treatment of cancer itself. Sometimes a surgeon will perform an operation to remove the tumour, and that may be the only step required. But, many patients may need other treatment, such as more specialized surgery, radiotherapy or treatment with chemotherapy (anti-cancer drugs). These are all specialized disciplines within medicine. Oncology is the study of tumours (the word derives from the Greek *onkos*, meaning bulk, mass or tumour) and an oncologist is a doctor who specializes in the treatment of patients with cancer.

THE ONCOLOGIST

To confuse matters further, there are different types of oncologists. A clinical oncologist is the broad term for a doctor who specializes in the care of cancer patients. A surgical oncologist is a surgeon. A radiotherapist – sometimes known as a radiation oncologist – is involved in radiotherapy, the use of X-rays to treat cancer. A medical oncologist specializes in the treatment of cancer with drugs.

Often a radiotherapist will be trained to use drugs as well.

Although cancer is common, many hospitals will not have a full-time oncologist. Instead, a cancer specialist may visit from a larger centre on a weekly, or less regular, basis to conduct a clinic and see patients. Within the hospital hierarchy, there will be a specialist responsible for your care — a consultant in the UK and a specialist, assistant or associate professor in North America. Underneath him or her there will be a team of doctors (including senior registrars, registrars, senior house officers and house officers in the UK, or fellows, interns or residents, in North America) in descending order of experience. In a cancer centre, all the doctors in the team will specialize in the treatment of cancer and will be training or fully accredited in that specialty. In smaller hospitals, the team may have a much more general function, dealing with many common illnesses within a department of medicine. If you are uncertain as to what is going on, and how specialized the team looking after you is, you should seek advice from the most senior person involved in the overall strategy for your care.

THE RIGHT TREATMENT FOR YOU

By the time you see a cancer specialist, a diagnosis will have been made. Drawing up a plan of your treatment is the next step. For many curable cancers it is vital that this plan is tailored to the individual. The best chance of cure lies in getting the correct treatment as early as possible.

The first thing cancer specialists will do is ask questions and examine you. They will then review the investigations that have been performed and perhaps request more. The reason for this is to get as full a picture as possible of you. You may have been more anxious when you first met the cancer specialist, and you may not have been as well as usual. The more accurate the specialists' impressions of you, the more likely they are to detect changes later, both during and after your treatment. They want to get as much information as possible about the tumour and you, so that your progress can be followed more readily. This may mean more blood tests, to look for substances produced by the tumour and secreted into the blood, or special X-rays, such as computerized tomographic scans (CT scans) or magnetic resonance imaging (MRI scans) to determine how big a tumour is at a particular site. If there is any doubt as to the diagnosis, you may even need a further biopsy, although fortunately this is extremely rare. Specialists use all this information to assess how far the disease has spread, and this process is called staging.

STAGING

Many systems for staging cancer have evolved over the last few decades. They are a useful way of comparing the results of different treatments in different centres. From studies which are published in medical journals it is possible to assess how you are likely to compare with others with disease of the same type and stage. Consequently, it not only enables treatment to be tailored more appropriately to our needs, but it gives an indication of what your chances of being cured are – information which every patient has the right to know and which an increasing number wish to know. Obviously, these are only statistics and you cannot see them as hard and fast rules, but they do give an indication of the probabilities of cure or recurrence. For patients with curable tumours, they can be reassuring, as cancer has a bad press and is far too often assumed to be terminal.

One of the most commonly used staging systems is the TNM system which was developed by a committee of the UICC (International Union Against Cancer – the initials stand for the French, Union Internationale Contre le Cancer). In this system the letter T stands for tumour (T1 implies a small tumour and T4 a very large tumour). Other numbers and letters are added to denote different sites of the body, e.g. N stands for nodes – the lymph nodes draining the organ in which the tumour is found. Enlarged lymph nodes, or glands, containing growing tumours are classified as N1, 2 or 3, depending on the size, site of the tumour and number of nodes. M denotes metastases (distant spread of the disease) which are either present (M1) or absent (M0).

By knowing the stage a cancer has reached, the doctor has a good idea of what the patient's chances of recovery are. An early stage (Stage 1) has a better chance of being cured than a late stage (Stage 3 or 4) of the same disease.

In most cancers the treatment will depend on the degree of spread. In Hodgkin's disease, for example, the disease can be treated with local radiotherapy if it is localized and at an early stage; but if it has spread to other areas, and is associated with symptoms suggesting systemic (or widespread) disease, chemotherapy is the usual treatment.

The specialist will also look at the information obtained from the initial biopsy. This will show not only the type of tumour and which category of a particular disease it is, but it will give an indication of the likely growth pattern of the disease. This is usually termed the grade of the tumour. This sort of information gives the doctor a very good idea of how a tumour is likely to behave.

The grade refers to the degree of malignancy (that is, how quickly a tumour is growing, or dividing). High-grade tumours are more abnormal and the cells divide more frequently. Consequently, they tend to grow rapidly, invade widely and are more likely to spread to distant sites. Under the microscope, they can easily be distinguished from the surrounding normal tissue. At the other end of the spectrum, low-grade tumours are relatively similar to the surrounding tissue, grow more slowly and are less likely to spread. They have relatively few cells which are dividing. Sometimes the grade of a tumour is given as a number – Grade 1 being of low grade and better outcome than Grade 4.

Most treatment of cancer depends on interfering with cells which are dividing – cells which are passing through the cell cycle and not quiescent. Hence chemotherapy and radiotherapy will be less effective in low-grade tumours, where only a small number of the cells are dividing, and there may be resistance to treatment.

Conversely (and perhaps paradoxically) high-grade, aggressive tumours, in which a great many of the cells are dividing, are likely to be more sensitive to treatment. Such tumours respond by shrinking rapidly, whilst low-grade tumours shrink more slowly. On the other hand, high-grade tumours can grow back much more rapidly. This is only a general rule, however, and there are frequent exceptions.

A combination of stage and grade provides the specialist with a fair idea of what is likely to happen, and can be used to decide on the best treatment for that particular patient.

An increasing number of patients are being treated privately, paying their fees directly or through a medical insurance company, and more and more employers use insurance schemes as a perk for senior staff. Although general practitioner care is usually through the NHS, tests to diagnose cancer may be performed privately. Then a decision has to be made about treatment. In the UK, and countries such as France and Germany, the national health service or health care system will cover much of the true cost of care, which is very high. Private health care, which is not paid for either by the State or a national insurance scheme, is very expensive. In the UK, the fact that the NHS is 'free' makes many of us undervalue its services. In Europe, the amount of money spent per year on health care is low in comparison with such countries as Japan and the United States, but the health care systems are surprisingly efficient. One reason for this efficiency in the UK is the general practitioner system, which provides an initial diagnosis and a suitable referral to a specialist, thereby streamlining patients into the relevant services, and preventing them moving between a series of inappropriate specialists in pursuit of advice.

In any of these countries, if you are not insured, then potential costs involved in the private diagnosis and possible treatment of cancer are likely to be extremely high and should be considered very carefully before incurring them. The most important thing about cancer treatment is that the best possible and most appropriate plan for therapy is drawn up, and that the correct decision is made at each step. The environment in which this is done is irrelevant. Many leading cancer centres operate in relatively primitive conditions, and many charlatans practice in elegant private health care institutions. It is very difficult for the consumer to know what is best.

The first thing to ensure is that your specialist really is a senior doctor in the field. Many doctors with minimal qualifications will practice as specialists in relatively unsupervised private health care systems. In the UK this means that it is important to ensure that your specialist has an NHS appointment as a consultant. Elsewhere, it is important to know whether somebody is working in isolation or whether there are a team of doctors, not only working under the guidance of this individual but also laterally within different sub-specialties of cancer. Doctors working within the field of oncology are likely to specialize in cancers in different sites of the body. In the course of your treatment you may be seen by several doctors, some of whom will be learning their specialty. Surprising as this may seem, it actually allows for more safety. Young doctors are more questioning, and will discuss problems eagerly with their senior colleagues. Hence, there will be a greater pool of knowledge from several sources. Ultimately, the treatment is very likely to be similar in a number of different centres — it is the process of arriving at that decision which is important.

There is another argument in cancer care, particularly topical in the UK, which is about the importance of centres of excellence of an adequate size. There are many small units in many Western countries, staffed by one or two specialists who may indeed be near to retirement and not up to date with the latest methods of treatment. Equally, the equipment may be antiquated. If you are concerned, ask your GP (or the doctor who has made the initial diagnosis) to refer you to a larger centre, such as one associated with a teaching hospital. Oncology is what is known as a tertiary referral specialty. This means that many patients will come from general hospitals in more provincial districts to larger, more specialized hospitals, perhaps in a metropolis which may be associated with a university. The travelling distance may be greater but, if there is a possibility of cure, and that possibility is increased by being dealt with in a specialist centre, it is obviously worth it in the long term.

GETTING INFORMATION

Just as we are all different in all sorts of ways, we all need different amounts of information about our disease. Some patients are content to leave it to the doctors to get on with their treatment plan, and may not even want to know if they have cancer. Indeed, some go as far as denying they have cancer, even though they have been told the diagnosis on several occasions. They are unlikely to be reading this book! Other patients, perhaps some of our readers, will want to know everything down to the last detail, and will wish to be involved in treatment decisions. Doctors have now come to respect patient preferences, and most cancer specialists have an open mind, answering questions honestly and as best as they can. But, to get the information you want, you must know what to ask. Many people are unfamiliar with the workings of a motor car, but are quite happy to nod wisely whilst a mechanic explains in technical terms, and come away with only a vague idea of what is wrong. As long as it can be fixed at a reasonable price, does it matter anyway? But if you or a close relative or friend has cancer, there is more at stake than a car; after all, a car can always be replaced.

This book will give you a good grasp of the processes involved in cancer care. If you are diagnosed as having cancer, you will want to know what type of tumour it is, what the primary site is – that is, where it originally started – where it has spread, its stage and perhaps other information which can give you clues as to the likely chances of being cured. Do not be afraid to ask – some doctors will not volunteer much information unless probed by the patient. There are still physicians who adopt a rather paternalistic attitude, patting their patients on the back and telling them not to worry. This may also cover up a doctor's ignorance and their indecision as to what to do. It may even be covering their own difficulty with the diagnosis. Probe for the answers. We know from experience in the clinic that patients who ask will receive information, and those who do not may not get it. Many young doctors training in oncology are very good at explaining things to patients. But if you are not getting the answers to your questions, or are not confident about the responses being given, ask to see the senior specialist; he or she is responsible for your care.

We have made a list of questions which you might like to use. We would stress, however, that it is much better to get them answered during a free-flowing discussion, rather than sit in front of your specialist with a structured interview and a list of questions before you. Some patients find it helpful to bring recorders to tape the doctor's replies so that they can be listened to again at home. When the diagnosis of cancer is first mentioned, people are often too shocked to ask questions. But cancer treatment is not usually started immediately, so there is plenty of time to think things through and come back with questions.

CHECKLIST OF QUESTIONS

- *What type of tumour is it?*

- *How big is the primary tumour?*

- *Has it spread to the lymph nodes?*

- *Has it spread anywhere else in the body?*

- *What stage is the tumour?*

- *Are there any indications from the pathologist, and are they good or bad?*

- *What treatment do you propose to carry out?*

- *Where will this treatment be done and who will be responsible for it?*

- *Will I have to go into hospital and, if so, for how long?*

- *What are the side-effects of any drugs that I might need?*

- *How often will the drugs be given and for how long?*

- *What are the chances of my tumour being cured?*

- *If it cannot be cured, could you give me a rough idea of my life expectancy?*

There is insufficient space in this book to go into great detail about specific tumours. But, in the last section, we list a number of sources where useful information can be obtained on individual cancers. In addition, cancer information services, such as BACUP and Cancerlink, will provide excellent booklets on particular cancer types. These can be used to help you frame the questions you want answered. As we keep stressing, the quality of information received is up to you. The patient is in a stronger position than ever to have his or her demands met. The attitudes of health care professionals have changed in recent years, and patients are now widely considered as clients within the system.

SECOND OPINION

Doctors may disagree, and have done so since the time of Hippocrates. The reason for this is that medicine is still an art rather than a precise science: there are always a number of ways in which the same result can be achieved. Cancer medicine is no exception. Many large centres have case conferences where individual patient problems are discussed and a body of opinion will be formed. There is regular disagreement on even the most simple decisions, such as whether to recommend post-operative radiotherapy, or how many doses of chemotherapy should be given after an operation.

If you are happy with the information you have received, all well and good; but if you are not, you are entitled to obtain a second opinion from another specialist. There is an unwritten rule in medical practice in the UK that patients are not seen by specialists without a request from their GP. The reason for this is clear. If you turned up to see another specialist having had a series of investigations and perhaps a biopsy performed elsewhere, the second specialist would have to start again unless they had the results available. The information which many patients have about their condition may not reflect the actual situation because of misunderstandings and inadequate communication. To obtain a valuable second opinion, all the information must be laid in front of the specialist.

In the US and many other countries the system is different. Second opinions are often initiated directly by the patient and are much easier to obtain. Such opinions can be expensive, the doctor will insist on seeing all the X-rays performed, and will obtain biopsy material for review by his own pathologist. This may seem a little extreme, but in difficult cases it may be the only way to obtain a worthwhile consultation. In the UK it is essential that a letter from the GP, stating the problem, is obtained, perhaps with a copy of the summary of the first specialist. Ideally, you would want the first specialist to co-operate and pass on all the information which he or she had at that time, both to avoid duplication and to speed-up the process. No doctor of any standing will be offended if you ask for a second opinion. We all understand the complexity of modern medicine, and no single person is infallible. The outcome of a diagnosis of cancer and the attendant treatment, be it surgery, drugs or radiotherapy, can result in a complete change of lifestyle. So, feel free to ask for a second opinion.

GETTING THE FACTS FROM YOUR DOCTOR

- *Make a list of questions you want answered.*

- *Do not be afraid to ask anything – the doctor will usually respond truthfully.*

- *Make sure you know what alternatives are available.*

- *Take a relative or close friend with you – you can then discuss the answers afterwards.*

- *Taking a cassette recorder may be helpful, but it is rather intimidating for the doctor – the answers you get may be much more guarded.*

- *Discuss any queries with your GP.*

- *If you are not happy about any aspect of your treatment, tell the doctors.*

- *Ask to see the consultant, or specialist, responsible for your care if you are unhappy.*

- *Nurses and radiographers are a very useful source of information.*

CHAPTER FIVE

Surgery

S urgery is the oldest form of treatment for cancer. The Greeks and Romans were skilled at tumour removal, and sometimes cured patients with what would have been a very primitive operation. There were no anaesthetics or antiseptics. Antibiotics to prevent post-operative infection were undreamed of, and the chances of an operation being successful were therefore minimal. Nowadays things have changed. Surgery has become a scientific discipline in which detailed knowledge of the structure and functions of the body, along with advanced technology, has resulted in many operations being possible which could not have been performed before. Similarly, many once major operations are now being conducted as day-case surgery through much smaller incisions – keyhole surgery, as it's called.

The aim of cancer surgery is to remove the whole tumour, whilst leaving behind as much normal tissue as possible. The cancer surgeon has to perform a balancing act. The tumour must be removed in its entirety for the operation to be a success; but if at the same time much normal tissue is removed with the tumour, the patient may have serious problems later. Progress in cancer surgery has come from knowing, confidently, how much tissue needs to be removed. The history of breast cancer is an excellent example of this.

BREAST CANCER

The most usual symptom of breast cancer is a lump in the breast. Most lumps are small, usually under 5 cm in diameter and yet, in spite of their small size, they may spread throughout the lymphatic channels into the lymph nodes (glands) under the armpits, or around the body into the neck and across the chest into the opposite armpit. Small clusters of cells may break off and be carried in the bloodstream to the bones, liver, brain and lungs; areas where breast cancer cells like to grow. Different tumours behave in different ways and, despite increasing scientific information about the sites of these secondaries (or metastases), we are still unable to predict how a tumour will behave in any individual patient.

Until the late nineteenth century, breast cancer surgery was a crude affair and used only for the worst types of tumour, well beyond cure. In 1890, William Halstead, an American surgeon working in Baltimore, pioneered an operation which still bears his name – the Halstead radical mastectomy. Mastectomy means removal of the breast. Halstead believed that by removing the whole breast, along with the lymph nodes under the armpit and a significant amount of underlying muscle, he would be able to encompass the whole tumour and its likely sites of spread.

For many years, the Halstead mastectomy dominated the treatment of breast cancer around the world. It appeared logical that by removing the lymph nodes, at the same time as the tumour, survival would be improved. At the time pathologists could actually see clusters of breast cancer cells in the removed lymph nodes. Surely this must be the best treatment? But removal of the main muscle of the chest left women with considerable disfigurement. The whole chest became lop-sided with one side being concave. It was difficult to correct this completely with any form of prosthesis (prosthesis being the name for an artificial breast in this instance). The lymphatics were often damaged, so that the arm on the same side would swell up, become thickened and brawny in appearance and very difficult and uncomfortable to use. All this, even though the patient was cured of her disease.

Unhappy with the results, several surgeons in the 1940s decided to try modifications of Halstead's famous operation. They no longer removed most of the main muscle covering the ribcage. Many years later, the results of this new operation were compared to the Halstead procedure and found to be the same. The new operation was widely adopted.

At the same time, Geoffrey Keynes, a radiotherapist working at St Thomas's Hospital, was pioneering work with radioactive implants. His results suggested that mastectomy might not be necessary in all patients. In the 1950s radiotherapy improved still further with the development of new higher-energy machines to deliver radiation – linear accelerators and cobalt units. For the first time, radiotherapy could be given in a predictable and tailored manner, following the contours of the body and without causing excessive damage in areas receiving the highest dosage. A number of clinical trials were established to see whether radiotherapy to the chest wall and lymph nodes draining the breast would be of any value after radical mastectomy.

At the same time, surgeons began to experiment with more conservative treatments. The next operation was the simple mastectomy, which involved removing only the breast but not the muscle underneath or the lymph nodes. For women with a small lump and no evidence of disease in the armpit, this produced exactly the same results as the radical mastectomy. In the early 1970s this was the most commonly performed operation. There was much controversy about whether radiotherapy should be given after simple mastectomy. We now know that, unless the tumour is large (at least 2 cm in diameter) or the lymph nodes contain disease, radiotherapy may not be necessary.

The next stage was for some surgeons to do what would once have been unthinkable, remove only the tumour and leave the normal breast around it intact. The operation was termed a 'lumpectomy', and afterwards patients were given radiotherapy with a small booster dose to the tumour bed. Comparing results of this surgery and radiotherapy with patients who had received other types of treatment, the number of women surviving was exactly the same. Women who have received conservative therapy (lumpectomy, or sometimes called quadrantectomy), followed by radiotherapy, are usually very pleased with the outcome. Psychologically, many women prefer to be left with apparently normal breasts. However, individuals vary very widely, and the options should always be fully discussed with the doctor responsible prior to surgery. Given the choice, Nancy Reagan chose mastectomy. At best, the only cosmetic change visible, in the case of a lumpectomy, might be absence of hair under the armpit on the irradiated side. With a small lump and a skilled surgeon it may be difficult for the doctor in the follow-up clinic to tell which breast has been treated.

Many studies involving patients have now shown the wisdom of a conservative surgical approach. This may not seem very logical, but the fact is that lymph nodes do not act as a barrier to breast cancer spread. However radical the surgery, it cannot deal with small clumps and numbers of cells which have spread to other organs of the body via the bloodstream. This spread may already have occurred in spite of removing the lymph nodes, and if that is the case the disease will recur whatever surgery or radiotherapy has been given. It therefore makes perfect sense to move to more conservative treatments.

Not all patients are suited to a lumpectomy. A patient with small breasts and a large tumour may be better treated with mastectomy. Attempting to preserve the breast simply as a matter of principle may give them a poorer cosmetic result than the simple diagonal scar after a simple mastectomy. If the breast remnant is without a nipple because the tumour was underlying the nipple area, the cosmetic result of mastectomy may again be preferable. It may also be easier to wear a prosthesis comfortably after simple mastectomy than an extensive lumpectomy.

As a patient, it is your right to know exactly what is going on, and why a particular course of action is being taken. Your surgeon may not be the best communicator. Once again, we urge you to ask what is happening. After all, it is your body. For every operation a consent form must be signed. It will outline that the procedure to be carried out has been fully explained to you. Do not sign it unless you are happy that this is the case and that you have received adequate information.

COLO-RECTAL CANCER

Cancer of the colon, like breast cancer, is a common disease. It is called colo-rectal because most colonic tumours lie at the lower end of the colon, which blends into the rectum – the external opening of the bowel. Colo-rectal tumours may result in symptoms which include blood in the stool, the production of excess mucus, occasional abdominal pain and sometimes diarrhoea. The doctor is likely to ask you if you have had a change of bowel habit, and if this is the case it should be reported so that problem can be investigated.

Tumours which lie high up in the colon, broadly speaking right-sided colonic tumours, can be removed through an operation in which the abdominal wall is opened from the front, the tumour cut out and the pieces of the intestine joined back together. This procedure is called an anterior resection (literally, cutting the tumour out from the front). There is a greater problem facing the surgeon when the tumour lies at the lower end of the colon, or within the rectum. If the surgeon is to remove the disease, he may have to take a margin of tissue which involves destroying the mechanism which controls bowel movement. The standard procedure for these operations was to perform a colostomy, to remove the affected bowel and without conserving the anal sphincter. The patient was left with a colostomy bag. Most patients adapt readily to this, and support is given by paramedical staff to help the adjustment. Nevertheless, a new piece of surgical equipment has resulted in a higher proportion of patients being spared the need for a colostomy. The surgeon can cut the tumour away at the lower end of the colon and then, using a staple gun, join the two ends deep inside the pelvis – one of many examples of how technology has moved on and facilitated more conservative surgery.

BONE TUMOURS

Bone tumours are relatively rare, although they occur in young adults and children. They are most likely to arise in the leg. In the past, the practice was to amputate the limb above the level of the tumour and then treat treat the patient with combination chemotherapy to destroy any small clumps of tumour cells which may be left behind. This is obviously very disfiguring, and particularly unfortunate in young people. For many years this has created an impetus to find alternative, more conservative, approaches. Orthopaedic surgeons, with the support of technical developments, have been able to experiment with removing simply the bone containing the tumour and replacing it with an artificial bone which may be able to expand as the child grows. These developments are still relatively novel, but they have progressed rapidly in recent years. The need for children and young people to have mutilating surgery and the loss of a limb for the rest of their lives is likely to be far less frequent in future. A greater understanding of the role of radiotherapy and chemotherapy and how best they can be combined will enable the long-term outcome to be the same and better than it once was with amputation alone.

THE OPERATION

Having an operation for cancer is really like any other. You are usually admitted to hospital a day before for last minute investigations, although increasingly frequently this may be done in advance, and you will be admitted on the morning of surgery if there is no prior preparation necessary, as there might be with bowel surgery. Your general condition will be assessed to make sure you are fit to tolerate an anaesthetic. This means excluding a chest infection and any other factors that might make your recovery more difficult post-operatively. The first doctor you are likely to see is the house surgeon. He or she is the most junior member of the team and will ask you questions about your general health, give you a thorough examination and organize the necessary tests. You may then be seen by the anaethestist who will double check that you are fit to have an anaesthetic and are not on any medication which might interact with it.

On the day of the operation you will receive an injection or tablet known as pre-medication, which will make you feel more relaxed before being taken to the operating theatre. In an ante-room outside the theatre the anaesthetic is first administered. This is completely painless and not unpleasant – a simple injection into your arm will send you to sleep within a few seconds. The trolley on which you lie will be wheeled into the operating theatre, and the operation begins. After your operation you will spend some time in the recovery area where your heart, pulse and breathing are monitored closely to make sure you have recovered fully from the anaesthetic. Once you come round you will be taken back to the ward.

The number of days spent in hospital will depend on the type of operation carried out, and your general medical condition. The removal of a breast lump may only require overnight admission; indeed, in some centres it may be possible to perform it as a day case. More major surgery, such as a major abdominal operation or the removal of a lung for lung cancer, are likely to mean staying in hospital up to two to three weeks. In the past decade it has become evident that more patients do better if they are discharged soon after surgery. It is important that they are encouraged to be up and about as quickly as possible, and return to being mobile and back to their daily routine as soon as they feel fit. This is greatly encouraged, and in-patient stays have dropped dramatically in the past few years without any risk to patients. Indeed, the risks of staying in bed too long, such as developing clots in the veins of your legs, chest infections or even post-operative wound infections, far outweigh the short-term discomfort and tiredness of being discharged promptly. It may be at this stage, after your surgery, that you will meet the specialists who may need to administer radiotherapy or chemotherapy at the next stage in your treatment. Before you leave hospital it is important to ensure that arrangements have been made for follow-up. Some patients may require no further treatment, but most will return to the clinic on a regular basis for check-ups, and some may have particular investigations.

PLASTIC SURGERY

The advent of new surgical techniques, microsurgery, laser and keyhole surgery has enabled less invasive operations to be performed and has thereby reduced the morbidity of surgery for cancer over the years. In addition, the same and similar techniques have enabled the development of improved plastic surgery with better cosmetic results. Consequently breast reconstruction is now more frequently performed, and the level of patient satisfaction continues to rise. If you feel you may benefit from plastic surgery, whatever your original operation, your oncologist can arrange for you to speak to a plastic surgeon about the possible advantages and disadvantages. Each case must be considered on its own merits, and you will need to be fully informed in order to make the right decision for you.

CONVALESCENCE

This really means protracted rest, sitting around relaxing, perhaps even getting bored. As we have already pointed out, it is preferable for patients to be up and about and resume their normal activities as soon as possible. Cancer surgery is no exception. For this reason, many of the convalescent homes which were once associated with hospitals have disappeared. We now have better anaesthetics, better facilities, better support services and less invasive ways of performing surgery, all of which facilitate an early discharge from hospital and a quick resumption of normal routine. Convalescence is now something which you organize yourself, and may simply mean being sensible if you have a very physically active job, and taking advantage of other people's support.

THE FUTURE

It is unlikely that any surgical advance will result in increased cures for cancer patients. On the contrary, it is new techniques which provide images of tumours and give an indication as to how far they have spread which will enable us to define the boundaries of a tumour more accurately, and thereby minimize damage to normal tissue. Developments, such as computerized tomography and magnetic resonance imaging, have already improved our ability to delineate tumours more accurately. With more developments, which might include the use of scans involving tumour-specific markers or better scanning to look at the blood supply of a tumour, it is likely that cancer surgery will become a much more precise science.

Another development which has been watched with great interest by oncologists is organ transplantation. It is logical that, if disease is present in the liver, then complete removal of the liver followed by a transplant, could cure the patient. Sadly, the results of liver, kidney, pancreas and lung transplantation in cancer patients have been disappointing. If the tumour is so large that the whole organ needs to be removed, it is likely to have already spread to other parts of the body. For this reason it is unlikely that transplant surgery will offer increased hope in the future. Instead, targeting radiotherapy and drugs to cancer cells, and thereby sparing normal cells following operations, is more likely to increase the number of patients cured. The dramatic improvement in the results of a variety of childhood cancers where surgery is used to remove the tumour is one pointer to the future for adults. The single most important factor here is a greater understanding of the role of combination chemotherapy with the integrated approach whereby surgery is used to remove the bulk of the tumour and followed by a combination of radiotherapy and chemotherapy to eliminate any remaining cancer cells. We are now seeing a higher proportion of such patients being cured, and those who are cured suffer less morbidity.

SURGERY – THE FACTS

Most patients with cancer will have some sort of operation, even if only a biopsy.

SURGERY: WHAT YOU NEED TO KNOW

- *The aim of cancer surgery is to remove the whole tumour, leaving behind as much normal tissue as possible.*

- *There is a great deal of controversy about the best type of surgery for particular cancers – be sure that you understand the alternatives.*

- *The period of convalescence after surgery varies enormously.*

- *If you are likely to have to meet some of the expenses, make sure that you understand the costs and the full implications.*

- *Do not sign a consent form unless you are entirely satisfied that you understand what is happening.*

CHAPTER SIX

Radiotherapy

Radiotherapy, as a form of treatment for cancer, cannot be considered in isolation. The vast majority of patients with cancer will require surgery at some point, and this may entail a simple biopsy or a major operation. In addition, chemotherapy may well form part of treatment either before, during, or after radiotherapy. This combined approach is important and, with greater experience and improved methods of treatment, has produced better results and an increased chance of survival.

Radiotherapy is the administration of X-rays, which were discovered by Wilhelm Röntgen in 1895. Within a year of their discovery they had been used in the treatment of cancer. We have come a long way since then. The use of radiotherapy to treat cancer is becoming increasingly sophisticated.

WHAT IS RADIOTHERAPY?

The first apparatus for therapeutic X-ray production was invented in the early part of this century by an American named William Coolidge. The principles have not changed greatly since. A heated metal filament produces a beam of electrons which is directed towards a metal plate. When the electrons strike the plate, part of the energy they lose is converted into X-rays which are diverted at high speeds. The amount of energy carried by the X-rays depends on the force with which the electron beam hits the plate, and this can be altered. The greater the energy of the X-rays, the further they can penetrate into tissue.

Laboratory evidence suggests that radiotherapy works by damaging the DNA in the nucleus of each cell. DNA is a structure which consists of two intertwined helices. The various parts of the DNA molecule are arranged in a particular sequence – a vital code for proteins which have important functions both inside and outside the cell. Radiation breaks the backbone of the molecule and, when the strands join back together, this vital code is altered. It is these breaks in the DNA which result in a cell's death. It may be possible for the cell to divide once or twice after being exposed to radiation, but eventually all the cells which have been exposed will stop dividing and disintegrate.

Radiotherapy aims to damage malignant cells irreparably, whilst limiting the damage to normal tissue in the surrounding area. Tumour cells, which usually multiply more frequently than the surrounding normal cells, seem to be more sensitive to radiation and also less likely to be able to repair the damage caused. We have learnt how to exploit this and establish a fine balance between tumour control and damage to normal tissue. In deciding how much radiotherapy to give to a particular tumour, doctors have to set the benefits of treatment against the risk of developing complications. The problem with this approach is that for any particular individual not only can the risk of complications vary but also their acceptability. For example, a change in the character of the voice following treatment of cancer of the throat will be of greater concern to an opera singer than to a butcher.

DIFFERENT TYPES OF X-RAY TREATMENT

The wonders of modern radiation therapy have only been achieved through a process of trial and error which began early this century. X-rays were discovered through their ability to blacken photographic film and 'X' was used by Röntgen to stand for 'unknown'. The early low-energy X-rays produced dramatic responses in skin cancers where results were easy to see. This led to the use of radiotherapy in a wide range of conditions, including tuberculosis, peptic ulcers and skin diseases. Although these conditions were untreatable by any other method at the time, a proportion of the patients died as a result of an X-ray overdose, and many suffered needlessly. We now know that highly penetrating X-rays, if not monitored and kept below a limit, are far from harmless; and for this reason radiotherapy is rarely used except to treat malignant disease. Yet, as recently as the 1950s it was possible to have feet X-rayed in a shoe shop to establish whether shoes fitted. It seems inconceivable now, but it was even possible for a child to sit on his pregnant mother's lap whilst having his scalp irradiated for ringworm! Throughout this period the greatest successes from the use of radiation therapy were seen in the treatment of cancer.

From the outset there were two complementary approaches to treating cancer. One was to use an external radiation source (either X-rays produced by a machine or a radioactive source held at a distance from the patient), and the other a form of treatment where the radioactive source was placed inside the patient. The latter involves implanting radioactive materials (which emit radiation spontaneously as they decay) into the tumour in the form of needles or similar devices. Alternatively, a container with the radioactive source inside may be placed within a cavity such as the uterus – this is known as interstitial or intracavitary radiation (*see Figure 6.1*). The use of implanted radioactive sources has been particularly effective in the treatment of cancer of the womb and cervix. In early cancers it may be the only necessary form of radiation, although more commonly it is used in addition to external beam radiotherapy to give an extra high dose in the immediate area surrounding the tumour.

The first radioactive source used for the treatment of cancer was radium. More recently, however, radium has been replaced by other sources, such as caesium, cobalt and iridium. These are preferable, both in terms of their powers of penetration, and also in that there is no risk of inhaling radioactive gases. The dose

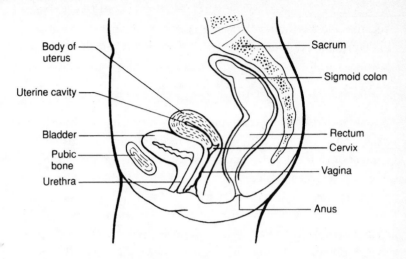

Figure 6.1 *A cross-section through a woman's pelvis showing the relationship of the uterus and vagina to the bladder in front and the rectum behind.*

received by the public and staff at a distance from the patient is relatively small. Increasingly stringent rules governing radiation mean that those who come into contact with the patient will only be exposed to a minimum risk. Any risk should be taken seriously, but current knowledge suggests that the chance of such a small radiation exposure resulting in illness or death at a later stage is extremely small (far smaller than the risk of cancer from living with a smoker). The only exceptions are in the exposure of pregnant women, or children under the age of about 12. Children and unborn babies are particularly susceptible to the effects of radiation, and their access to wards where radioactive sources are present is restricted. Improvements in the last two decades mean that many of the unwanted effects of treatment seen with older, less powerful, machinery are now a thing of the past. Indeed, with the advent of a computer for planning as well as CT scanning, it is possible to treat a localized deep-seated tumour with only a slight early skin reaction and no apparent long-term cosmetic side-effects in the form of broken blood vessels or skin fibrosis. This is because the high-energy beams currently available are able to penetrate the body more effectively.

WHO IS IN CHARGE OF YOUR TREATMENT?

When you are actually receiving radiotherapy you will be seen on a daily basis by the radiographers or radiation technologists. They are responsible for setting up the machines, ensuring that the correct dose is given and consulting the doctors if they are unhappy about any aspect of your general health during treatment. The importance of accuracy here is so great that at least three radiographers will be involved. They will be at varying levels of experience and expertise, with one radiographer taking overall responsibility for a machine. Radiographers are highly qualified individuals who have had at least four years' training and many years of experience before they are promoted within the hierarchy. They are very knowledgeable, and provide a valuable point of contact on a day-to-day basis.

You may not meet the physicists during your treatment, but they play a key part in any radiotherapy department, not least in checking machines and providing the doctors with the information they need on the distribution of the dose. The physicist also helps the doctor decide what form of treatment should be used, given the size and location of any particular tumour.

In spite of occasional adverse publicity, radiotherapy is a remarkably safe form of treatment. There are very clear guidelines on the calibration of machinery, and it is a legal requirement for the machines to be checked frequently.

PLANNING

Having decided which treatment is best, the next stage will be to plan it in detail. It is at this stage that you will make your first trip to the radiotherapy centre. X-rays and scans will be taken to determine where the X-ray beam should enter your body. Planning is then carried out on a machine known as the simulator – a machine which literally simulates your treatment on the X-ray therapy machine and can produce X-rays like those used for making a diagnosis. The position of light beams will then be marked on your skin with a pen. When treating complicated areas where marks are unsightly or less likely to stay, a Perspex shell may be made which is contoured to fit that part of your body. The main purpose of this is to prevent you moving during treatment so that the X-ray beam touches only those tissues it is meant to touch. Holes are cut out of the shell so that your eyes, nose and mouth are not covered, and marks showing where the X-ray beams should penetrate can then be made on the Perspex. Careful notes are kept so that the position of the X-ray beam is the same on each visit you make. Indeed, nowadays, a Polaroid photograph is likely to be taken when you first attend for planning so that the therapy radiographers can reproduce this position accurately when you have your treatment.

There are standard treatments for certain cancers, but these have to be modified to take into account factors such as your shape, physical mobility, general health, age, sex, the cosmetic result required, and even the distance you have to travel for treatment. No two individuals are the same. So don't be alarmed if you compare notes with other patients with the same disease and discover that their treatment is different from yours. There are all sorts of reasons for this, ranging from the stage the disease has reached to your personal circumstances – such as whether or not it is convenient to stay overnight in hospital. If you are at all concerned by anything, ask your doctor.

When you first attend for planning, you will meet at least one doctor and probably more than one radiographer. Don't be afraid to ask questions about your particular treatment and any fears you may have. In this section there is a list of questions that you may want to ask when starting radiotherapy.

WHAT IS IT LIKE TO HAVE RADIOTHERAPY?

Once the doctors, radiographers and physicists are satisfied that the treatment prescribed is appropriate and practical, the treatment will be carried out. The machine used may be a linear accelerator, a machine containing a radioactive source such as cobalt or caesium, or a superficial X-ray machine (used for skin cancers). These are often found in the basement of the building. The machines lie in lead-lined rooms which are built to protect the radiographers and staff outside the room from receiving more than a tiny dose – usually less than one-millionth of the dose prescribed for the patient. Different centres will have different machines available, with large centres having a wider choice. It may be suitable for the patient to be treated at a smaller centre nearer home which does not necessitate long hours spent travelling to and from the hospital each day. Once again, a balancing act is performed between the needs of the patient with regard to treatment and their quality of life. You should be fully involved in this decision and must ask the doctor any questions which would influence it. If the most important aspect of the treatment is the cosmetic result, then this may necessitate a lengthy treatment given at a relatively low dose rate in the hope of avoiding long-term damage. However, if the final appearance is not of concern, but other factors are more important (such as a disabled spouse being left alone for long periods during the day), then a short course of radiotherapy at a higher dose rate (that is, given in fewer, larger doses over a shorter period of time) may be more appropriate. Radiotherapy is flexible and it is important that the patient makes his or her needs apparent at the outset, so that the doctor can tailor the treatment appropriately.

RADIOTHERAPY CHECKLIST

- *When will the treatment be planned?*

- *How long will planning take?*

- *When will the treatment start?*

- *How many treatments will I have, and how long will they last?*

- *Will it be every day, or how often per week will it take place?*

- *Can I drive myself and, if so, where can I park my car?*

- *How much flexibility is there about transportation or the time of treatment each day?*

- *Are there any days when I will not be treated – such as public holidays?*

- *Are there any immediate side-effects?*

- *What should I do about them?*

- *Is there anything to avoid – e.g. sunbathing, swimming, washing?*

- *How often will I see the doctor?*

- *What happens when my treatment is completed?*

CURE OR CONTROL?

It is important for people to understand why they are being given radiotherapy. It may be intended as a complete cure – this is known as radical radiotherapy. It may be being used to decrease the likelihood of the tumour coming back at the site of origin. A third, and very important, use of radiotherapy is palliation – to control symptoms. As a general rule, courses of palliative radiotherapy tend to be shorter.

Radiotherapy may be given as an alternative to surgery. In head and neck cancer, for example, surgery may be more disfiguring than radiotherapy. A good example of this is in cancer of the larynx. The surgical treatment of this condition would involve removing the larynx and, as a result, the patient would have to learn to speak without vocal cords. The use of radiotherapy, although it may influence the character and quality of the voice, usually enables the voice to be preserved, and as a result has a lower morbidity. Radiotherapy may be used after surgery, as in the case of breast cancer; and it may be used before surgery to reduce the size of the tumour so that the operation does not have to be so extensive. In each of these situations, the aim is to reduce the number of cancer cells. Where a cure is hoped for, this would leave no cells capable of forming a further tumour.

The aim of radiotherapy is to treat patients so that the tumour is damaged as much as possible while the normal tissue is spared. People who are potentially curable will be treated 'radically' to ensure the best possible cosmetic result, and the maximum sparing of normal tissue, whilst giving the greatest chance of tumour control. At the other end of the spectrum, the patient who is unlikely to live for a normal period of life and may indeed only be expected to live for weeks or months, will be treated 'palliatively' to control the symptoms. Doctors have to strike a balance between the need for treatment, the time involved and the likely remaining life span.

Most tumours are treated with radical radiation over a period of five to six weeks. This is certainly true of tumours in head and neck, abdomen and pelvis. Four to five weeks' treatment is usually adequate for particularly sensitive tumours such as lymphomas, or particularly radio-resistant tumours such as melanomas, where large doses of radiotherapy at each fraction or session of treatment are thought to be more effective. One important form of palliative radiotherapy is the 'hemibody' (i.e. half of the body). This can be used to treat patients with widespread secondary spread in the skin or bone, where pain is likely to be the main symptom. The patient is admitted to hospital, and the area to be treated determined. This may be the lower half of the body from the navel to the knees, or the upper half from the navel up to the neck. The patient usually receives a sedative and an anti-sickness drug and, if the lower half of the body is being treated, a drug to prevent diarrhoea. The treatment is given as one single large dose to the relevant half of the body, and the patient remains in hospital overnight for observation. This form of treatment can be very effective, with a dramatic improvement in pain and discomfort, quite often within as little as 24 hours.

GENERAL ADVICE

- *Ask questions of the radiographers and doctors you encounter during your treatment. Your relationship with medical staff is likely to be a long one, and misunderstandings may mean that it gets off on the wrong footing. Questions may not arise during the planning of the treatment, but in most centres there will be a weekly clinic where you will have the opportunity to discuss any problems.*

- *If a particular side-effect seems severe, do not play it down. If the staff are not informed, then appropriate investigations cannot be carried out, nor tablets be prescribed to alleviate symptoms.*

- *Be prepared to be adaptable and to take rests. It may be necessary to take time off work, to avoid frequent or prolonged breaks in your treatment and to get plenty of rest. Having started a course of radiotherapy, it is important that the time over which it is given is approximately the same as that which was intended. One day off to visit the Palace for your knighthood would be perfectly acceptable! Longer breaks may be unavoidable for personal reasons, but if they can be anticipated it is worth mentioning them at the outset – it may even be preferable to start the treatment slightly later, or tailor it to incorporate the outside commitment in some way.*

SIDE-EFFECTS OF RADIOTHERAPY

One side-effect which many patients experience during their treatment is general fatigue and tiredness. This is to be expected, and you should not be surprised if you need an extra two to three hours' sleep per day. Other than that, early side-effects tend to relate to the area being treated. If you are having a small area treated, particularly on the limbs, you are unlikely to experience much in the way of side-effects. At worst, your skin may be slightly red and sore towards the end of the treatment (like a localized sunburn) but nausea, diarrhoea and lethargy are extremely unlikely. Only the area being treated is likely to be affected by the radiation. The exception to this rule is the haemopoietic system (put simply – your blood). Your blood is circulating around your body during treatment and, as a result, any red or white blood cells which pass through the treatment area may be damaged. In the majority of patients, this is of no significance, but where a large area is being treated over a long period of time, or the patient has had or is currently having chemotherapy, the number of white blood cells, which fight infection, may be reduced, thereby increasing the risk of infection. Your doctor is likely to point out this problem during treatment, and monitor your blood count more frequently.

Individuals vary in their sensitivity to radiation. The same dose may produce a severe skin reaction in one person and only a mild reaction in another. As a rule, the symptoms are worst towards the end of treatment, and often reach a peak after four to five weeks. Nausea may be noticed at the beginning of treatment, but gradually improves with time. This may be experienced when a larger part of the body is treated. Nausea is particularly common during treatment to the abdomen, although it may also be experienced by patients having treatment to nearby structures.

Side-effects depend on the dose given, as well as on the size of the area being treated. With the advent of high-energy radiotherapy, treatment of a deep-seated tumour does not entail a particularly high dose to the skin, and many patients in this category will have only a minimal skin reaction. Conversely, treatment to an area such as the breast does involve a reasonably large dose to the skin, necessary because the breast itself lies just beneath the skin. Here, there may be quite marked soreness towards the end of the course, particularly in areas of skin folds, such as just under the breast or into the armpit. One of the most difficult regions to treat is the head and neck area. In order to give a dose sufficient to control the tumour with minimal damage to tissue at a later stage, the treatment is likely to produce severe soreness of the mucus membranes which line the inside of the mouth and the throat. As a result, swallowing may become temporarily painful and difficult. Medication is readily available to help alleviate the symptoms, and there are certain simple measures, such as avoiding alcohol and spicy foods, which will also help.

LONG-TERM SIDE-EFFECTS

For each individual the significance of long-term side-effects will vary. In young people, infertility may be a very high price to pay, whereas later in life loss of hair may be the most demoralizing aspect of treatment. It may be possible to overcome some of the long-term side-effects in other ways: in a man, for example, infertility may be overcome by storing sperm. For a woman, the possibility of being left infertile may mean choosing between surgery and radiotherapy as the primary method of treatment. Again, you have every right to discuss the possible long-term side-effects with your doctor at the outset, so that you can decide together on the emphasis of your treatment and which side-effects, if any, can be avoided. The benefits must be set against the price paid. Cure at any cost may not be justified. This may well be the case in an older patient who feels that he or she has already lived a fulfilled and happy life, and is not prepared to accept the possible consequences of invasive and disfiguring surgery or radiotherapy.

Hair loss after radiotherapy is only a problem when the head itself has been treated. In the vast majority of patients it is not permanent, and regrowth will start from as little as four to five weeks after treatment. If the patient has a slow-growing brain tumour, the dose to certain parts of the scalp may necessarily have been very high. This may result in permanent damage to some of the hair follicles, and consequently thinning of the hair at a later stage. However, the advent of CT scanning and linear accelerators means that the scalp can often be spared, leaving the patient with a reasonably thick head of hair in the long term.

Only treatment of the pelvis with radiotherapy will bring about infertility. This may be temporary. Treatment of one testis can be carried out with lead shielding to the other, thereby preserving fertility. The treatment of pelvic tumours in women by radiotherapy may be an alternative to surgery. In cervical cancer, surgery is used for early disease in younger women, in order to conserve the ovaries and avoid thickening of the skin of the vagina (which makes intercourse painful). Any woman who is considering having a child after treatment should consult her doctor. Women on hormones, or who have recently completed chemotherapy, are usually advised to avoid becoming pregnant in the short term. Again this is an area where our experience is growing daily, and it is important that all the possibilities and implications are discussed fully between you, your family and the doctor.

A much more common late side-effect, experienced in varying degrees, is the long-term cosmetic outcome of your radiotherapy. A good illustration of this problem is the treatment of breast cancer after removal of the tumour. If the patient feels that the cosmetic result is not important to her, the treatment can be given in a small number of large doses with gaps between the treatment from a few days up to one week. The tumour control is comparable to that achieved using five- to six-week courses of daily radiotherapy. On the other hand, treatment spread out over five to six weeks, with small daily doses to the breast followed by an extra dose to the scar area, is more likely to result in good control of the tumour and a good cosmetic result. The breast is likely to remain softer and the skin finer. In elderly patients, who have difficulty in travelling to the cancer centre, and whose life expectancy may only be a few years simply by dint of their age, once-weekly treatment may be more appropriate. With the treatment involving smaller daily doses, it may be difficult to tell which breast has been treated months later when the skin reaction has settled. A number of methods can be used to give the extra treatment to the breast scar: these include electron beam therapy (a different type of radiotherapy, which treats only the 2 to 3 cm below the scar); a radioactive implant (which may be inserted under a general anaesthetic, after which the patient remains on the ward for a few days); or a reducing field technique whereby the whole breast is treated initially, and then the area of the breast in which the tumour is located is given further doses, which gradually reduce in size to encompass only the tumour bed itself.

The cosmetic outcome of all these treatments is controversial – some physicians feel that top-up with a radioactive implant provides the best cosmetic result; others feel that electron beam therapy, given on an out-patient basis, is more convenient and does not entail the inevitable risk of a general anaesthetic, with comparable cosmetic results. The long-term cosmetic appearance will only become apparent over a period of months and years after treatment when the patient is followed up. Firmness in the breast, often particularly evident around the area of the scar where the top-up was given, may only be obvious one or two years after treatment, and may become more apparent over the subsequent years until it reaches a static point. For many patients this is not a major problem. The most important aspect is that when they go to the follow-up clinic they are reassured that this is a normal occurrence.

THE LIMITATIONS OF RADIOTHERAPY

Tumours are given a dose of radiotherapy which is close to the maximum tolerated by the normal tissues in the region. The risk of damage to normal tissue is the major factor limiting the use of radiotherapy and, for this reason, radiotherapy is only used to treat cancers which are localized (i.e. have not spread) at the time of treatment. Should the tumour recur, further radiotherapy would exceed the normal tissue tolerance and the patient might well suffer severe side-effects – possibly fatal – from damage to such sensitive tissues. Sensitive structures include the brain, spinal cord, lungs, liver and bone marrow. It must be frustrating and sometimes incomprehensible when a tumour shrinks away after radiotherapy, that the same tumour cannot be dissipated a second time by the use of further radiotherapy. Both radiotherapy and chemotherapy damage the source of rapidly dividing cells in the bone marrow, and eventually the body may no longer be able to produce enough white blood cells, platelets and finally red blood cells. The amount of bone marrow treated by radiotherapy will subsequently limit the amount of chemotherapy which can be given for a particular disease. As a result of this restriction, no form of radiotherapy or chemotherapy should ever be given without seriously considering the immediate effect and the long-term consequences.

MYTHS ABOUT RADIOTHERAPY

Do You Lose Your Hair?

A common misconception is that radiotherapy inevitably causes hair loss. Radiotherapy can only cause hair loss if the scalp is within the area being treated. Similarly, axillary hair will be lost if the armpit is being treated, but not otherwise.

Do You Become Radioactive?

During radiotherapy, the part of your body being treated is exposed to radiation. This is in much the same way as when you have a chest X-ray, although the radiation is of greater energy. The rays pass through you during the treatment with the intention of killing cancer cells within that area. The only way in which an individual can become radioactive during radiotherapy is to consume a radioactive drink – this is sometimes used as a treatment for an overactive thyroid, or for thyroid cancer itself, when radioactive iodine is drunk. You may also be radioactive transiently if you have a radioactive implant inserted into you as part of your treatment. In each case you will be told that you are radioactive, as you will not be allowed home with the implant, and after the drink you will be monitored until you are safe to be discharged. Treatment with radiation from a machine, however, which accounts for the vast majority of patients receiving radiotherapy, does not make you radioactive.

Can You Wash During Radiotherapy?

One of the most upsetting aspects of treatment is the advice not to wash during therapy. Indeed, one study actually showed that this was one of the worst problems which patients experience. This general piece of advice which is bandied about often restricts patients from having baths or showers unnecessarily, and a few well-directed questions can avoid the misunderstanding. Washing with cool or lukewarm water and dabbing yourself dry gently are perfectly acceptable and, if the area being treated does not need to get wet in the bath, there is no reason why the rest of your body cannot be bathed normally. It is also possible to gently shampoo the head weekly with a mild shampoo and no friction, even when this area is being treated. The most important thing is to be sensible; the skin overlying the area being treated can be splashed with cold or lukewarm water, but it should not be scrubbed or rubbed dry, and creams should be avoided. It is all a matter of degree, but you do not have to feel unhygienic during your treatment.

Towards the end of your therapy, the skin will become increasingly red and sore and friction will exacerbate this problem. Using creams on your skin actually increases the dose of radiation to the skin surface, as the cream acts as a form of 'build-up', making the redness and burning worse. Once again, you should ask the radiographers' advice, and alternative ways of relieving the symptoms may be suggested.

THE 'FACTORY' PROBLEM

The cost of radiotherapy machinery and the number of staff involved in the treatment process mean that radiotherapy centres are usually widely spaced geographically. It may be necessary to travel long distances to receive an adequate service, and the large busy departments may be rather impersonal in comparison with a visit to your GP's surgery. This is particularly demoralizing if you are only just coming to terms with a diagnosis of cancer. Some people are able to use this experience positively, deriving strength from the feeling of camaraderie and mutual experience of other patients. The nurses, radiographers and doctors are another important resource to be utilized in increasing your own understanding of the process of radiotherapy and its rationale. It is only through this insight that the fear and perceived lack of control, which may result from the disease and its treatment, can be avoided.

FOLLOW-UP VISITS

Once the initial radical treatment (that is, the treatment which is intended to cure you) has been completed, you will visit the hospital regularly as an out-patient to be checked by a member of the team which looked after you. Initially this was to check whether your skin, which looks very sunburnt after treatment, has returned to normal and, where possible, to assess your response to that treatment. In many cancers this takes the form of a 'wait and see' approach. You may have had investigations before and during radiotherapy to assess the extent of your disease. These may include X-rays, scans and blood tests. At this point the important distinction for both you and your doctor is whether the disease is confined to the primary site, or has spread outside this region. There is no guarantee in any patient that there are not microscopic clumps of cancer cells outside the primary site. Unless these are at least 5 mm in diameter they will not be reliably detectable with any of the currently available technology.

Initially, your follow-up visits will be relatively frequent – probably every two to three months. As time goes by, these visits will become more spread out, and may be six months or a year apart. The period of follow-up is variable and there are no hard and fast rules. If you find out-patient attendances upsetting, and feel you can take responsibility for noting symptoms or detecting any changes, it may be reasonable for clinic visits to be kept to a minimum – with the proviso that you re-attend the clinic if you are in any way worried about new developments. Most cancers carry a 99 per cent chance of being cured if no symptoms have recurred after 5 years. This is particularly true of head and neck cancers, lung cancers and some sarcomas. However, most patients are followed up for up to 10 years. With diseases such as the lymphomas, there is a small risk of second malignancy. For this reason most lymphoma patients are followed up for life. Breast cancer is in a different category, and even 20 years after the primary treatment it is not unknown for a patient to develop secondary deposits. Such late recurrences often respond well to hormone therapy, and it may be feasible to prolong a patient's life for many years. Indeed, it may not actually be the cause of their death ultimately.

The understanding that you can return promptly to the clinic if you have any worries or fears, or that your GP can seek your consultant's advice at a later stage, should anything unexpected happen, means that recurrences can be detected early and consequently are more readily treatable. The follow-up clinic is a useful time to ask any questions, to express any fears and to seek reassurance about any late side-effects which may have arisen. Without an explanation from the doctor at such a time, these problems, particularly unexpected ones, might otherwise be very alarming.

CASE HISTORY

Miss D was a medical student who noticed a sore on the roof of her mouth at the age of 20. When sampled, this revealed a melanoma (a tumour arising from the pigmented cells of the skin). There was a hole in the centre of the tumour which connected back with the cavity behind the nose. Because of the position of this tumour and the number of vital structures close to it, it was important that as much normal tissue as possible was spared. To ensure this, treatment was carried out with radiotherapy from six different directions, with two directions being treated at any one time. During treatment the hole closed up, the sore healed and, apart from minimal soreness at the roof of the mouth, there were virtually no side-effects. Within four weeks of treatment the redness had resolved completely and only a small indentation was visible. Some years later she had no problems in spite of the usual very poor prognosis. More important, extensive disfiguring surgery had been completely avoided.

This case history shows how radiotherapy can sometimes have an advantage over surgery. It also demonstrates that with the technological advances of the last decade the side-effects of radiotherapy are not what they were, indeed they are being mitigated all the time, and it is not a form of treatment to be feared.

CHAPTER SEVEN

Chemotherapy

W e have seen in the previous chapters how cancer can be treated effectively by surgery or radiotherapy when it is localized to a particular site in the body. Unfortunately, the main problem with cancer is that it spreads – first along the lymphatic channels to nearby lymph nodes, and then on into the bloodstream and beyond into other organs. Surgery and radiotherapy can only deal with local disease. When spread has taken place, the treatment which has to be given must be systemic. That means it has to circulate around the body, reaching any sites wherever the cancer cells may be.

Until 1944 there was no known drug effective against cancer. At the end of the Second World War, the US military began experimenting with new chemical weapons. They came across the alkylating agents — drugs which bind to DNA, the vital code which is present in every cell. Basically, these agents completely destroy the mechanism whereby DNA produces its message. The first of these agents was nitrogen mustard, and many other related compounds were subsequently discovered.

During field trials, in which volunteer soldiers were exposed to the alkylating agents on military manoeuvres, it was found that the white cell count in the blood fell dramatically. This prompted Lewis Goodman, an American pharmacologist, to use one of the alkylating agents, mustine, in a patient with lymphoma. (A lymphoma is a tumour of the lymph nodes.) Goodman's patient also had a raised white blood count as a result of tumour cells spilling over into the blood. To everyone's amazement, the blood count fell and the patient's enlarged lymph node shrank rapidly after just one injection of mustine. The drug had unpleasant side-effects, causing very severe nausea and vomiting shortly after its administration, but the shrinkage of the tumour was dramatic. Several patients went through this new treatment for cancer amid great excitement. But then it was noted that many patients did not actually respond. Only those with lymphomas and leukaemias had dramatic improvements in their condition. Even here the disease started to grow again in between courses of mustine. Patients could only tolerate the drug in small amounts, as it was found to be very poisonous to their normal bone marrow, resulting in abnormal bleeding. It also suppressed the patient's innate defence mechanisms against bacteria, leading to an increased risk of infection.

But although the initial optimism was unfounded, a breakthrough had been made: a systemic drug was available for the treatment of cancer. Since 1945, more than 100 drugs with anti-cancer effects have been discovered, and about half are used routinely in cancer therapy. Drugs work via a number of different mechanisms. Some are useful in a range of different cancers, whereas others are very specific for the tumours which they can control. Some drugs work at the level of DNA, preventing it from being copied – a vital process in cell division. These drugs bind directly to DNA itself, distorting its structure and preventing the attachment of the enzymes necessary for it to copy itself and enable two new cells to be produced from one. Other drugs deplete the cell of the building blocks for DNA so that fewer raw materials are available for DNA replication. Still other drugs prevent binding of enzymes to produce RNA, the message made by translating this thread of life, which is vital in the production of proteins – the executive molecules of the cell. Drugs have been devised which block protein synthesis, essential for maintenance of cell activity and also for its division. From the periwinkle plant, *Vinca*, is produced a family of drugs collectively known as the vinca alkaloids. These block cell division by preventing small bundles of intracellular muscles from pulling chromosomes apart at the time of cell division.

THE DISCOVERY OF ANTI-CANCER DRUGS

The majority of anti-cancer drugs which we use were discovered by accident. Few were designed specifically to inhibit tumour cell growth.

In the 1950s, the National Cancer Institute in Washington, the largest cancer research enterprise in the world, embarked on a very ambitious programme of testing a whole range of sub-stances. Scientists collected chemicals from all over the world and all sorts of sources, and tested them for their ability to kill cancer cells. This programme uncovered a variety of structures which we still use to this day. Over a million compounds have now been screened, and vast banks of data collected via this process have been accumulated in the archives of the NCI.

There are more romantic stories about the discovery of anti-can-cer drugs. Several pharmaceutical companies developed pro-grammes to search for new drugs in fungi and algae, looking for a repeat of the famous penicillin story of Alexander Fleming. High by the Adriatic Sea in Northern Italy is an old tower built in medieval times. The tower itself is a crumbling ruin overgrown with moss and ivy. Samples of fungus were taken from this beau-tiful tower, and a drug which interfered with DNA, by inserting itself within the base pairs of DNA, was identified. This drug was found to be remarkably effective in controlling breast cancer, non-Hodgkin's lymphoma and a number of other tumour types. The drug is doxorubicin, given the brand name of Adriamycin, as it had been discovered on the Adriatic coast.

The discovery of cisplatin, commonly used for testicular cancer, sarcomas and gynaecological tumours, is another interesting story. In the early 1960s, an American scientist, Bill Rosenberg, was interested in the ability of electrical fields to inhibit bacterial growth. He was a pure scientist working in a laboratory, with no intention of developing new anti-cancer agents. His experimental system was relatively simple. He grew bacteria in a small dish and measured how many would grow in a defined period of time. He then inserted two electrodes and passed an electric current between them. He noticed that the growth rate of the bacteria diminished when the electric current was switched on. Initially, he came to the conclusion that the electric current inhibited bacterial cell growth. Being of an enquiring mind, he performed the following experiment. He took food from bacteria which had been inhibited by the passage of an electric current and added it to fresh bacteria. Much to his surprise, he found that the growth rate of the second batch of bacteria was also diminished, even though no electric current had been passed through. A substance was produced by the passage of electric current which inhibited cell growth. This substance was found to be soluble platinum, produced by the passage of electricity through the platinum electrodes used in the experiment. Platinum is a precious metal used for jewellery and several industrial purposes. Although familiar as a shiny, grey-silver metallic solid, its organic form is a white crystalline powder. Cisplatin was the first of a series of platinum-containing complexes which were found to have considerable effect on particular tumours. A chance observation had given rise to a new group of anti-cancer drugs.

The initial discovery of alkylating agents, a group of drugs widely used in the treatment of leukaemia and lymphomas, led to the screening of many other drugs that would bind to DNA. Some drugs were designed to increase their solubility or their ability to concentrate in tumours. Drugs have also been modified to try to reduce side-effects. Cisplatin, for example, has very profound side-effects on the kidney. It causes irreversible damage to the small tubes of the kidney, with subsequent renal failure. To avoid this, patients are given a large amount of fluid by intravenous infusion both prior to and after the administration of cisplatin. This means that patients usually have to spend some time in hospital. Carboplatin, a drug with a similar structure, is less damaging to the kidneys and avoids the need for hospital admission. Unfortunately, carboplatin is more likely to damage the bone marrow, and its most important side-effect is a low white blood cell and platelet count. This usually occurs approximately two weeks after its administration and is described as the nadir. The next cycle cannot be administered until the blood count – white blood cells, red blood cells and platelets – has risen to an acceptable level.

SIDE-EFFECTS

Because tumour cells are so close in structure and function to normal cells, it is not surprising that any drug which reduces cancer growth also affects normal cells. This means that many drugs have powerful side-effects. For this reason, they are usually only prescribed by specialists in the field. Consequently, GPs and other hospital doctors are not involved in cancer drug administration on a regular basis as it can be very dangerous, indeed potentially lethal, in unskilled hands. Anti-cancer drugs inhibit cell turnover generally and so the most rapidly dividing cells in the body – the bone marrow, lining of the intestine, skin and hair follicles are most severely affected.

In the skin, itching can occur and hair loss is common. Some drugs are more notorious for causing hair loss than others. Adriamycin is the drug most likely to have this effect. Although attempts have been made to reduce hair loss by putting elastic bands around the scalp, or cooling the scalp during the period when the drug is being given, none of these methods is completely effective. The effect on the bone marrow results in a decline of the red cells (leading to anaemia), the white cells (leading to a decrease in leukocytes and depressed resistance to infection) and thrombocytopenia when the platelets (tiny factors in the blood which are vital for clotting) are depleted. Anaemia can easily be corrected by blood transfusion; but thrombocytopenia can result in abnormal bleeding into body cavities, or to the exterior. To avoid problems of bone marrow depression, patients having chemotherapy have a blood test to check their blood count and kidney function before the next course of chemotherapy can be given. The dose and number of drugs given can then be adjusted if necessary. Some drugs cause the cells lining the intestine to switch off, which leads to severe diarrhoea and fluid loss. Suppression of the immune system is common with anti-cancer drugs. This decreases the defence against infection, and patients may be more susceptible to sore throats and other unpleasant symptoms. Patients having chemotherapy are regularly checked by the physicians for infection. Any signs of it are dealt with rapidly by using appropriate antibiotics. Another curious effect of many anti-cancer drugs is that they can cause specific changes in single organs. For example, Adriamycin in large quantities is toxic to the muscle of the heart, resulting in circulatory problems in a few patients. Similarly, bleomycin causes fibrosis in the lung. This can cause shortness of breath or shadows on a chest X-ray. Cisplatin can cause kidney damage. Several other drugs result in pigmentation. For this last reason, some patients on long-term anti-cancer drugs may look more pigmented than usual.

Part of good cancer management is trying to administer drugs, and combinations of drugs, in such a way as to maximize their effect on the tumour and yet minimize their effect on normal cells. In most cases, we believe the best way to do this is to give the drugs in large doses at intervals of three to four weeks. This enables the bone marrow to recover in between. Tumour cells are not so well able to repair the damage caused by the drugs as their normal counterparts. One of the major problems in the treatment of particular cancers is resistance to these drugs. It is thought that giving several different drugs at the same time in large doses will kill tumour cells before they have a chance to develop resis-tance. Those cells resistant to one drug may not be resistant to another which acts via a different mechanism. This is thought to be an important aspect behind the effectiveness of combination chemotherapy. The other advantage is that the side-effects and toxicities of drugs which act through different mechanisms are likely to be different. Consequently the dose of one drug will not be limited by that of another. This enables relatively higher doses of each to be given than would be possible with a single drug.

One side-effect which is often neglected is the psychological effect on a patient, and his or her family, of repeated hospital visits, often with much waiting around for the results of investigations, including blood counts and, in some cases, unpleasant nausea and vomiting. The latter are caused by the effect of chemotherapy directly on the lining of the stomach and on an area which lies at the back of the brain. This zone is responsible for sea sickness. Certain types of irregular swinging motion cause signals to be sent from the inner ear to this zone, known as the vomiting centre, and this induces sickness in some patients. This varies very widely from patient to patient. Some drugs may cause severe vomiting in one patient and yet not affect another. Fortunately, there are a variety of drugs available which prevent this vomiting. These can act in a number of ways – increase stomach emptying, suppress the vomiting centre directly and confuse the brain into thinking all is well, or simply suppress the memory. Perhaps the most interesting is a drug called nabilone. This is a synthetic derivative of cannabis or marijuana. It was noted, in the flower power days of the 1960s in California, that patients who smoked pot were not sick during chemotherapy. The same effect was noticed with those who consumed 'hash-brownies'. Hash-brownies are little brown chocolate cakes into which marijuana is mixed before baking. Some patients like the mild hallucinogenic effect and the dreamlike trance which seems to stop the sickness caused by the chemotherapy. Nabilone is a synthetic cannabinoid (it is made in the laboratory) which is similar to marijuana, but it does not cause the associated hallucinations. It is not suitable therapy for all patients' sickness and it generally appears that older patients do not like the slight feeling of loss of control associated with nabilone. But in younger patients it may be very effective when other compounds fail.

A patient who suffers from severe vomiting with chemotherapy, may need to be given anti-sickness drugs before actually attending hospital to have chemotherapy. This type of nausea and vomiting is known as anticipatory, and may arise from associations with the experience of receiving chemotherapy. This is explained by the phenomenon of conditioned reflexes and the story of Pavlov's dogs. Pavlov, a pioneering Russian psychologist, studied salivation in dogs. He noted that when dogs were given meat they would salivate and drool if they were hungry. He rang a bell just before giving them meat. After a period of time, the dogs learnt to salivate in response to hearing the bell, even if they were not about to be given meat. This process is called conditioning. We are all subject to conditioning from the day we are born. Vomiting when undergoing chemotherapy is a similar response: if a patient is violently sick the first time he has chemotherapy, he is likely to associate the two; he expects to be sick, and so he is. If this first unpleasant experience of vomiting can be prevented, then serious vomiting is less likely to take place later. In extreme cases a patient can actually start to feel sick when he sees anything associated with his chemotherapy. This might be watching a film about hospital life on television or, even more bizarre, such as when he sees his doctor at the supermarket on a Saturday morning.

Fortunately, there are now more powerful anti-nausea drugs available so, it is hoped, conditioning will be a thing of the past. There are also drugs which, in addition to having a small anti-nausea effect, have an important and useful sedative effect. The best and most widely used example of such a drug is lorazepam, which is more commonly known as a sleeping tablet. It has the advantage of reducing the recollection of events and consequently, even if the nausea experienced at the time is very severe, it is likely to reduce the possibility of recalling this experience, and therefore the likelihood of conditioning. Lorazepam is usually used in conjunction with other anti-sickness drugs.

The management of chemotherapy-induced nausea and

vomiting has been revolutionized in the past few years with the development of the 5-HT3 antagonists. These drugs, of which there are three major ones on the market, act by binding specifically to receptors, in that part of the brain called the vomiting centre, which are responsible for symptoms of nausea and vomiting. As we understand the processes behind these symptoms better, so we are able to treat them more effectively with new drugs.

Alongside this improvement in the treatment of chemotherapy-induced nausea and vomiting there has also been an improvement in the number of drugs which can be given on an out-patient basis. This is partly because our treatment of nausea and vomiting has improved, but also some new drugs do not need the precautions which require patients to stay in hospital, such as giving the patient fluid intravenously before and after treatment. One corollary of this is that some of the nausea and vomiting experienced by the patient occurs when they are at home, a few days after treatment. This is called delayed nausea and vomiting, and in some patients it can be a serious problem. Unfortunately the new 5-HT3 antagonists are not particularly good at treating this condition. If, as a patient, you experience symptoms four or five days after treatment, having had an initial improvement, make sure your doctor is informed before your next cycle is administered. They may be able to improve the situation with combinations of other drugs.

HOW ANTI-CANCER DRUGS ARE GIVEN

There are many ways in which drugs can be taken into the body and, of course, this applies to those which act against cancer. Some can be taken as pills or capsules. Unfortunately, many anti-cancer drugs are complicated and would be damaged inside the stomach or intestine or broken down with the food we eat. For this reason, many are given by injection into a vein. Some, such as mustine and Adriamycin, cause tissue breakdown when concentrated. To prevent this they have to be diluted by running the drug into a fast-flowing intravenous drip with other fluids, so that the drug is carried away into the bloodstream and diluted as it goes. To reduce the side-effects, some drugs are diluted into a bottle or bag of fluid, which is hung up as a drip leading into a vein.

Most anti-cancer drugs can be given in the out-patient clinic. The patient arrives, a blood sample is taken for the blood count to be determined, and the patient is seen by a doctor to check that all is well. If the blood count result is satisfactory, the doctor will prescribe the course of chemotherapy which is then obtained from, and usually made up by, the pharmacy. Some combinations of drugs use a mixture of tablets and injections. These combinations have been found by trial and error to be the best for that particular disease. Here are some examples of drug combinations which have brought about cures.

Lymphomas

Lymphomas consist of Hodgkin's disease (about 40 per cent) and non-Hodgkin's lymphoma (60 per cent). The latter are broadly divided into low-grade and high-grade tumours. Low-grade tumours are just that: they cause symptoms from time to time and these tend to respond to mild treatment often in tablet form. High-grade tumours used to be fatal but, using similar drug combinations to those used in Hodgkin's disease, a proportion have now been cured.

Hodgkin's Disease

Until 1965, the majority of patients with this disease died. Only those with a tumour localized to a small area which could be effectively treated with radiotherapy were cured. Hodgkin's disease is a lymphoma – a cancer of the cells which make up the lymphatic system. These lymphocytes are part of the blood's white cell complement and vital for defence against infection by bacteria and viruses. Doctors tried using new anti-cancer drugs in patients with lymphoma as soon as they became available in the mid–1940s. Although the drugs significantly reduced the amount of tumour present they did not eradicate it completely. Then, in 1965, the National Cancer Institute in Washington decided to treat patients with four drugs at the same time. Each drug was known to be of some help on an individual basis, and they hoped that the combined effects would produce a cure.

These four drugs – mustine, vincristine, procarbazine and prednisolone – were given over a fortnight. Two were given as tablets every day and the others by injection on the first and eighth day. Called MOPP, after the initial letters of the four drugs (the brand name of vincristine is Oncovin), the combination resulted in the complete and permanent disappearance of Hodgkin's disease from many patients. Many of those who received MOPP in 1965 are still alive today. Oncologists still use a very similar combination for the treatment of Hodgkin's disease.

This was a dramatic breakthrough. It led to new approaches combining existing drugs for a whole range of different cancer types. Over the next decade, four different types of cancer became curable in many patients – lymphoma, testicular cancer, choriocarcinoma and childhood leukaemia.

Childhood Leukaemia

More than 70 per cent of children with cancer can now be cured using a combination of surgery, radiotherapy and chemotherapy. The commonest, and most curable, childhood cancer is leukaemia. The treatment of children with leukaemia is carried out in a number of stages. The first stage is described as induction therapy. Patients are induced – they have intensive treatment over two to three weeks using four or five different drugs. The aim at the end of this time is for the patient to have gone into remission. In reality, 95 per cent of children have no evidence of leukaemia in their blood or bone marrow at this stage, that is they are in complete remission. After an interval, during which the normal blood cells can recover, the next phase is consolidation. The treatment may be consolidated with a further intensive programme of chemotherapy. Patients with a particularly poor outlook may have two periods of consolidation. Because many of the chemotherapy drugs do not cross into the fluid around the brain and spinal cord, patients also have to undergo radiotherapy to those areas to ensure that any leukaemia cells in the fluid are destroyed.

After this intensive period, the children can begin the third and final phase of treatment, assuming that they have responded up until this point. This is known as maintenance therapy – one drug on a daily base, another weekly and a monthly injection. The period of maintenance therapy is currently two years, although some patients with a good outlook, on the basis of particular prognostic factors, may have a shorter period of treatment. One important advance which has been made in the treatment of many childhood cancers in the past decade or so, and leukaemia is as good an example of this as any other, is the involvement of patients in large multi-centre trials. As childhood cancers are all relatively rare, it is important that patients undergoing novel therapies, or being involved in new changes of therapy which have not been evaluated, are treated within clinical trials. It is only in this way that we are able to make advances and make treatment for the next generation of children milder where they have a good outlook, and more intensive, and hence more likely to result in a cure, where they have a poor outlook. On this basis, it has become possible to remove the radiotherapy to the head and spinal cord, known as prophylactic cranial irradiation, from the treatment regimen of children who have a good prognosis or outlook and, by the same token, children who have a poor outlook are now more readily selected to undergo more intensive therapy, thereby increasing their chance of cure. There are many large national and international trials in childhood cancers and, as a result, cure rates have improved and morbidity has been reduced in this area more dramatically than any other. As an increasing number of children with childhood cancer are becoming long-term survivors it is important that side-effects such as infertility, growth stunting and the development of second malignancies, are avoided. This is happening as patients with a good outlook are having the chemotherapy or radiotherapy removed from their treatment. When this is undertaken within a clinical trial the risks can be defined and the group of patients compared with the previous generation.

Testicular Cancer

Until 1975 there was little chance that patients with widespread testicular cancer could be treated with chemotherapy. The response to single drugs was poor and lasted for only a short time. The combination of three drugs – cisplatin, vinblastine and bleomycin – dramatically increased the response rate. As with the paediatric cancers, over the subsequent few years, the treatment regimen has been modified to reduce toxicity, whilst retaining the high success rate. The most frequently used combination now is BEP – bleomycin, etoposide and cisplatin. Studies are currently in progress to determine the optimal number, and duration, of courses necessary to treat patients adequately. The doses of drugs are also being modified in patients with the best outlook.

In the majority of patients with testicular cancer, the response can be monitored in an accurate way by measuring proteins shed by the tumour into the blood, known as tumour markers.

In order to receive BEP, the patient is admitted to hospital. The drug carboplatin was mentioned earlier in comparison with cisplatin, in that it does not damage the kidneys and its administration consequently does not necessitate large volumes of fluid before and after the administration of the drug. Although JEB (carboplatin, etoposide and bleomycin; J stands for JM8, the brand name for carboplatin) is significantly more expensive than BEP, its administration is being more widely adopted as it does not necessitate an in-patient stay, and administration of an expensive drug as an out-patient is now as cost-effective as giving a cheaper drug which necessitates three to five days' in-patient stay. It is also widely accepted that the tumour markers are sufficiently accurate in teratoma, the type of testicular cancer where they are raised, that the number of cycles of chemotherapy given is simply two after the point at which the tumour markers have returned to normal. In most patients, four such cycles are sufficient to produce a cure.

Choriocarcinoma

This is a very rare tumour which arises from the cells of the placenta. The symptoms usually develop during pregnancy, with severe nausea and vomiting. Choriocarcinoma is sensitive to a similar combination of drugs to testicular cancer. Both tumours arise from cells involved in reproduction, known as germ cells, and they are sensitive to the same chemotherapy agents. As with childhood cancers, this rare tumour should be treated at centres with experience of the condition.

DRUG RESISTANCE

Drug resistance is perhaps the biggest problem in chemotherapy today. Although there has been great success in some cancer types, many common tumours are difficult to cure. It sometimes seems to be part of the behaviour pattern of the tumour from the start. For this reason, certain types of lung cancer are difficult to treat. Breast and ovarian cancer respond regularly to existing drugs, but become resistant within six months to a year in most cases. In some patients, there is drug resistance at the outset. Often the cells are resistant to a number of drugs. On a more positive note, there are some cancers, such as testicular cancer and Hodgkin's disease, which are not resistant at the outset and rarely develop problems, just melting away with successive courses of chemotherapy, in a predictable fashion.

But tumour cells are rather clever. They can adapt to unfavourable surroundings. They may do this by increasing their ability to destroy anti-cancer drugs by producing more of the enzyme required for their breakdown. Alternatively, they may develop special mechanisms to increase the export of, not just

SOME COMMON ANTI-CANCER DRUGS

Drug	Type of Cancer	How Given	Main Side-effects
Adriamycin	breast, lung, sarcomas	intravenously	alopecia, mild nausea
Bleomycin	testicular, lymphoma, head and neck tumours	intravenously, intramuscularly	lung fibrosis
Cisplatin	ovary, testicular, lung	intravenously	nausea, kidney damage
Chlorambucil	ovary, leukaemia, lymphoma	orally	bone marrow suppression, mild nausea
Cyclophosphamide	breast, lymphoma	orally or intravenously	bone marrow suppression, mild nausea
5-fluorouracil	colon, stomach, pancreas	orally or intravenously	redness of hands and feet, mouth ulcers
Methotrexate	bladder, breast, lung	orally or intravenously	mouth ulcers, kidney damage
Vincristine	lymphoma, childhood tumours, kidney, brain	intravenously	damage to nerves, numbness of hands and feet

Note: The side-effects mentioned above are not the inevitable consequence of taking these drugs. Most patients develop only mild problems. These are side-effects clinicians have to watch out for, and are more likely to develop after several cycles. The exception to this is probably nausea with cisplatin, but modern anti-sickness drugs have improved this situation greatly.

one, but several anti-cancer drugs at the same time. There is a molecule which actively pumps a number of drugs out of the cell. This sits astride the cell membrane. Tumour cells with large quantities of this molecule have evolved, and so show a survival advantage over those tumour cells without it. As the drug is exported from the cell, it is not able to inflict the damage which it must to kill the cancer cells. These types of cell, therefore, quickly multiply, and soon the tumour is made up of cells with an increased amount of export protein, and it consequently becomes drug-resistant.

Over the last few years, doctors have gained considerable insight into the molecular mechanisms of drug resistance, and it is hoped it will soon be possible to combat it or find other manoeuvres which decrease the chances of it arising. Drug resistance is one of the reasons why combination chemotherapy protocols, involving several drugs at the same time, have been devised.

MEDICAL ONCOLOGY

Medical oncology is the name given to the specialty concerned with the administration of anti-cancer drugs. Most doctors are not experienced in the use of these drugs. Indeed, many of them can only be prescribed in specialist units. The organization of the administration of chemotherapy varies from country to country. In the UK, a network of cancer centres of varying sizes is responsible for the care of most patients.

In the UK most chemotherapy is administered by doctors who give both radiotherapy and chemotherapy. Their title is consultant in clinical oncology, which was formerly known as radiotherapy. There are around 250 in the country. Medical oncology is a much smaller specialty, with only about 50 consultants. This is not true in most other Western countries, particularly Europe and North America where there are proportionately more medical oncologists. In these countries clinical oncologists are more likely to concentrate on treatment with radiotherapy alone.

In most centres, clinical oncologists (radiotherapists) and medical oncologists work closely together with surgeons and others to make sure the cancer treatment for an individual is the best possible.

In most countries, treatment in a larger centre is likely to be preferable, as the pool of expertise is greater. Even though it may be inconvenient to travel to another town for treatment, it is often worth while. Many specialists visit hospitals in surrounding districts in order to reduce the travelling time by the patient. As it has become possible to administer an increasing proportion of chemotherapy on an out-patient basis, and the skills of specialist nurses and nurse practitioners become more widely available, treatment is being given more locally in smaller hospitals. Only the therapy which necessitates expensive equipment (particularly radiotherapy), or specialist in-patient care, needs to be given at the larger cancer centres. Follow-up and out-patient therapy can be undertaken locally. This model – of the cancer centre as the hub and the smaller cancer units, with a visiting specialist, as the spokes – is being increasingly adopted throughout western Europe. In the United States, where you have the extreme of the free market, many individual doctors have established their own centres, without regard for the geographical distribution of patients, or the capital costs of such an exercise. Elsewhere, though, there is a more co-ordinated distribution of centres with the necessary expertise, and the hubs, and the rational distribution of spokes will follow where it is not already in place.

The danger area arises when the specialist fails to realize that he is no longer in touch with modern treatment regimens for a specific condition. This can happen at a time of change for the better in the results of treating a particular tumour type. A good example is the widely differing results obtained in different centres in the UK for the treatment of testicular cancer between 1982 and 1985. Some five years previously, the Americans had pioneered chemotherapy programmes containing platinum, and these should have been generally available within the UK. But the level of expertise varied enormously. During those years the mortality from testicular cancer at five centres, all within a 100 miles radius of each other, was compared. The centres treating more patients were clearly getting better results because they had the concentration of expertise to deal with particular clinical problems and were more aware of developments on a worldwide basis.

Another area where concentration of expertise is essential is children's cancer. Fortunately, cancer is rare in children and also amenable to expert treatment. Indeed, the response and cure rates are generally higher than in adult tumours. But treatment is often complicated, and needs the resources of a group of specialists dealing with the whole range of child-care problems. Treating the occasional child with leukaemia by looking it up in a textbook and copying out a drug regimen is a recipe for disaster. It is only by the concentration of resources and patients at centres of excellence that optimal care can be assured. This is vital for tumours where cure is a possibility.

Cancer is an emotive subject and, in comparison with many diseases, very newsworthy. This media interest serves to give it a high priority within health care, and the public is becoming increasingly aware of disparities in treatment and, at the same time, increasingly litigious. Fear of negligence, and better survival data is likely to facilitate comparisons between centres, making the treatment of cancer more homogeneous both within and between centres. In North America there are regular consumer surveys of different cancer centres, which not only look at aspects such as patient satisfaction and surroundings, but also survival statistics. Taken in isolation these are hardly useful, as they do not relate to the type and stage of disease seen at the cancer centre. Nevertheless, they are a powerful tool for change, and suggest that the days are over when uninformed, inadequately qualified individuals, could set themselves up to treat cancer.

GETTING THE RIGHT TREATMENT

If you do not take responsibility for this, why should anybody else? You are quite entitled to know precisely what plans your doctors have for your treatment in hospital. This book should help you understand some of the complex problems in treating cancer. A discussion with your own GP should put it in perspective. But, at the end of the day, it is the responsibility of those giving chemotherapy to explain how it will be done, the side-effects it might cause and the potential benefits. Nearly all those involved, whether nurses or doctors, will be happy to explain things which seem unclear. Some patients are afraid to ask, for fear of seeming stupid. Don't be. Keep asking until you are satisfied that you have enough information.

If you are still in doubt, you can seek a second opinion. As for surgery and radiotherapy, it is vital that the consultant giving an opinion has all your medical details and the proposed plan in front of him or her, otherwise he or she cannot arrive at a rational decision. For this reason, your GP or family physician should send a note detailing the situation, together with the results of any investigations. In this way a single consultation can be extremely useful.

CLINICAL TRIALS

Much of the treatment given for cancer is based on assumptions, and the accumulation of previous experience. Nevertheless, accepted therapies have not always been tested against alternatives, and consequently much of the practice of oncology is not fully tried and tested. Clinical trials are necessary to determine whether new drugs are effective or whether, when offered in combination, they have fewer side-effects than alternatives with the potential for destroying tumours. Clinical trials are an essential part of anti-cancer treatment. The advantages which clinical trial results bring have been illustrated in the section on childhood cancer. Much of the accepted wisdom in this field is based on the stringent testing of particular drug combinations, the best duration and intensity of treatment. In the more common adult cancers, where recruitment to trials is more difficult and the treatment likely to be more geographically varied, this is not always the case. Some of this may be for practical reasons – living in a rural area, the distances travelled will influence the number of treatments a patient is willing to accept; the patient's chronological and biological age will also be far more variable than in paediatric cancers. However, only by undertaking clinical trials can we improve on existing treatment. You may well be asked to join in a clinical trial. It is purely voluntary and there is no obligation. You are also at liberty to ask to be removed from the trial at any point if you are not happy about your management. A consent form will require your signature, and a full explanation of the study will be given. You should take this opportunity to ask anything else about your disease.

All clinical trials have to be approved by a hospital ethics committee consisting of doctors and lay people. This considers a wide range of ethical issues about the study.

Above all, an ethics committee will decide whether the new treatment proposed is likely to be as effective as existing treatment. If this is not confirmed by the results, there is a fail-safe system for stopping the trial at any point and switching to conventional treatment. As well as contributing to future knowledge, participating in a clinical trial can bring other dividends. You will be more closely monitored, and perhaps have more frequent checks on health and well-being than if not on a study. Most objections from patients arise because of misunderstandings. It's your body, so make sure you know exactly what is being tried and why. It may not simply be you, but many others may benefit as a result of your taking part.

CHAPTER EIGHT

Hormone Therapy

ormone therapy, also known as endocrine therapy, involving the use of hormones, small molecules normally produced by the body, can also be used to treat certain cancers. Hormones act as chemical messengers and are produced by endocrine glands. These glands include the pituitary at the base of the brain, the thyroid gland in the neck, the adrenal glands above the kidneys, the ovaries in women and the testes in men. Many hormones control the normal growth of particular tissues. For example, the female sex hormone oestrogen is produced in the ovary and stimulates the growth of cells in the breast. Changes in the relative levels of different hormones control the normal menstrual cycle and changes in the ovary and endometrium at the menarche and menopause.

In 1896, George Beatson, a Scottish surgeon, removed the ovaries from two young patients with advanced breast cancer. In both women, the disease stopped growing and regressed. Though the tumours later returned, this was the first demonstration that changing the circulating levels of hormones could be effective against cancer. We now know that the removal of the ovaries leads to a fall in the level of oestrogen in the blood. The amount of oestrogen reaching the breast tumour is therefore less, and the rate of tumour growth is reduced. Since Beatson's time, hormonal therapy has been widely used for cancers arising in tissue susceptible to hormonal influences – such as the breast, prostate and uterus. Just as hormones have been used in the treatment of breast cancer for nearly a century now, so they have been the standard form of treatment for cancer of the prostate, once it has spread beyond the prostate itself, for nearly 50 years. Oestrogens, or similar female hormones, inhibit the growth of prostate tissue.

There are a number of ways in which the level of hormone activity can be influenced. The first is to destroy the endocrine gland which produces it. The gland could be removed surgically, could be given a dose of radiation high enough to stop it functioning but sufficiently low not to cause damage to other surrounding tissues, or it could be tricked into switching off by a substance which mimics a naturally occurring substance. Alternatively, drugs could be used to block the effects of the hormones produced by the endocrine gland. This has the advantage of being reversible, but the disadvantage is that the patient needs regular drug administration – either by daily inhalation or by means of a depot injection under the skin which lasts for about one month – and it has a further disadvantage to the health care system in that it is significantly more expensive over a period of time. This means of treatment is more likely to be used in prostate cancer, and is only acceptable as third or fourth line chemotherapy in breast cancer as yet. The third approach is to give a hormone. Paradoxically, by giving very large doses of naturally occurring hormones, you may overwhelm the tissue which has developed cancer and the growth of the cells. Patients with breast cancer may consequently receive extra oestrogen. Alternatively, the hormone given may be one that the body would not normally secrete.

For hormones to work they have to interact with receptors in their target tissue. This can be likened to a key (the hormone) fitting a lock (the receptor). If another substance fits the same lock but does not activate it, the hormone's effect can be blocked. Such drugs are called anti-hormones. The best example is tamoxifen, which blocks the action of oestrogen, and it is often used in treating breast cancer. But, not all patients respond to hormonal treatment. Responses may be variable, even in cancers arising in the same tissue. Hormone treatment has relatively few side-effects. There is no bone marrow depression or hair loss. For this reason, hormones are often used as the main form of therapy in those tumours likely to be responsive.

Choice of therapy – be it removal of the gland, blocking the effects of the hormone or giving another hormone – will depend on the preference of the patient, a consideration of side-effects (some oestrogen therapy is not suitable in men with high blood pressure or heart disease) and expense. Tamoxifen has already been mentioned in breast cancer. Once a patient is no longer responding to tamoxifen, there are other hormonal therapies which can be used. These tend to be second or third choice as they have more side-effects, and as they are likely to be used as long-term therapy it is important that the treatment has as little impact on the patient's quality of life as possible. There is no evidence to suggest that the response achieved, or survival benefit, from one form of therapy is superior to another.

In breast cancer, the reason for responsiveness to hormone therapy is not completely understood. The effects appear to be dependent on the presence of receptors on the tumour cells. However, many of these receptors are measured and yet they still do not give a complete indication which tumours will actually respond when treated – some hormone receptor positive tumours do not respond, while some hormone receptor negative ones do.

Another phenomenon which is not fully explained is that of tumour flare. Patients given almost any form of hormonal therapy may experience new symptoms, or an exacerbation of old symptoms, within a few hours to a few days after starting treatment. These usually subside within a month. Paradoxically, patients who experience these side-effects are as likely to go on to respond to endocrine therapy as those who don't.

HORMONE THERAPY – CHECKLIST

- *Hormones act as chemical messengers and are produced by endocrine glands.*

- *The choice of hormone therapy will depend on a number of factors.*

- *Hormone therapy is widely used for cancers susceptible to hormonal influences, such as breast, prostate, uterus and ovary.*

- *There are a number of ways in which the level of hormone activity can be influenced — to destroy the endocrine gland which produces it; drugs could be used to block the effects of the hormones; or large doses of hormones could be given.*

- *Not all patients respond to treatment.*

3

Coping with Cancer

CHAPTER NINE

Complementary Medicine

*B*eing given a diagnosis of cancer is a traumatic and isolating experience, no matter how hard your doctor may try to soften the blow. Medical teaching in the past two decades has attempted to raise doctors' awareness of this but too little time and the hospital setting do not make things any easier. Many patients with cancer will die from it, and this is not something which anyone can accept lightly. Half of all patients admit to experiencing psychological and emotional problems and this may well be only the tip of the iceberg. Obtaining support at the outset, in the form of more information and counselling, may prevent much of this stress. Increasing numbers of cancer treatment departments recognize the need for psychological support and employ counsellors and psychotherapists, with formal training in this area, to help both in-patients and out-patients. Seeking help from a psychologist at such a difficult time is not something to be ashamed of. In addition, there are many self-help groups, helplines and cancer support groups. The links between such supportive care and the conventional delivery of treatment for cancer are beginning to strengthen, and an increasing number of departments have an established supportive care structure involving health care professionals from a range of disciplines. Others of the support and self-help groups are self-funded.

WHAT IS COMPLEMENTARY MEDICINE?

There has been a burgeoning increase in the availability of alternative treatments which may make the conventional cancer therapy, whatever it may be, more bearable. This treatment area has been termed complementary medicine.

Complementary medicine is just that – an attempt to complement and not thwart conventional care. Complementary medicine concentrates on the whole person, rather than just the disease, and is based on the belief that your attitudes and state of mind have a great influence on your physical health; if you are happy, relaxed and optimistic, then your physical health is likely to be better than if you are miserable and depressed. This approach to medicine is often used to treat diseases where health and resistance to infection are keys to recovery. Cancer is one such disease. Great emphasis is placed on self-healing and the wide range of therapies available means that most patients can find an acceptable option and, although diverse, they are usually harmless.

Most forms of complementary medicine start by looking at your lifestyle in general to see if there are any fears or psychological problems which may have a bearing on your present state. Of course, this does not mean that everyone with cancer has psychological problems which must be treated; but complementary medicine believes that, for your body to be healthy and able to fight disease, your mind must also be healthy.

The atmosphere of a hospital is often very hi-tech and impersonal, and many people find that this increases their anxiety. The result is that they find it difficult to communicate with the staff around them, and may bottle up their emotions until they are back at home in a familiar, comfortable atmosphere. This is where alternative or complementary medicine may come in. The problem with complementary medicine is that it is often difficult to find out what is available, the skills of the practitioners offering it and how much it will cost. In the past five years or so, it has been accepted more widely by the medical profession and, in cancer therapy in particular, is now seen as an adjunct to conventional treatment and is increasingly available within a department alongside these other therapies.

In the UK, one place where help is readily available is The Cancer Help Centre at Bristol, which has pioneered a well-organized approach that many have found very helpful. This was one of the first such centres in the world. It offers day- or week-long residential courses for patients and their carers. At the start of the week, counselling sessions with doctors and nurses help identify the type of treatment programme likely to be most beneficial to a particular individual. All sorts of complementary therapies, from special diets to healing, can be explored to find which best suits an individual's needs. Group sessions allow common problems to be shared so that a patient no longer feels so isolated. An atmosphere of peace pervades the centre, quite unlike most hospital wards or clinics. At the end of the week, day sessions are arranged so that the lessons learnt can be reinforced. Many people find themselves better able to cope with orthodox treatment after the support which they find from this experience. Many Western countries have similar centres, and some, such as the Gerson Centre in Mexico, have international reputations.

The organized approach available at centres of national or international repute certainly appears preferable to simply seeing the first local counsellor on the recommendation of a well-meaning friend. There is a world of difference between such organized and dedicated centres and many lone practitioners advertising their services as hypnotists, nutrition experts, reflexologists, faith healers and so on.

COMPLEMENTARY MEDICINE
– WHAT IS AVAILABLE

- *Counselling*

- *Acupuncture*

- *Aromatherapy*

- *Homoeopathy*

- *Herbalism*

- *Meditation*

- *Visualization*

- *Healing*

- *Relaxation*

- *Massage*

- *Osteopathy*

- *Reflexology*

- *Hypnotherapy*

- *Dietary treatments*

DIFFERENT PATIENTS' VIEWS

If you feel you would like to explore other methods of treatment in addition to conventional medicine, you must voice your needs, and ask about the complementary medicine available – that within the hospital itself, in the locality and on a national basis. The response you obtain is likely to vary from one consultant to another, but doctors are increasingly receptive to this approach and they are aware that patients have widely differing needs. Counselling in a hospital setting is becoming more widely available, and in this respect complementary medicine may well support medical and paramedical staff as patients find it a helpful way of coming to terms with the diagnosis of cancer and coping with conventional treatment. Indeed, caring for cancer patients carries its own stress, and staff may actually benefit from the availability of regular counselling themselves. Discussing difficult or upsetting problems related to patient care often helps to ease the burden. No two patients react in the same way to the diagnosis, and so their approach to treatment and their ability to carry on with their lives afterwards will also differ. Some want to abdicate responsibility to their specialists, others want to feel completely in control and, therefore, need as much information about their disease and its management as possible. Others have fixed ideas about their disease and its likely outcome, which no amount of persuasion can dislodge. Just as everyone will have a different approach to their illness, the help and information provided must be tailored to meet their individual requirements.

THE EXTREMISTS

A proportion of doctors within the NHS will be cynical about the use of complementary medicine but, by the same token, some complementary practitioners will pour scorn on conventional treatment. Both extremes are unhelpful for patient and doctor alike. They may serve to undermine your confidence in the treatment you have had (or are likely to be offered in the future), or compromise your relationship with the doctor offering conventional therapy if you bring the 'baggage' of the negative complementary therapist with you. Providing one form of treatment does not compromise the effectiveness of the other; it is best to be open -minded and receptive to both groups. For example, a patient receiving abdominal radiotherapy may insist on religiously adhering to a strict vegan diet which contains no meat, eggs, milk or cheese. The high intake of largely raw food contains much roughage and is likely to stimulate the bowel, making the side-effects of the radiotherapy much worse. There must be middle ground between these two approaches. It is probably in your best interests to be completely open to both conventional and complementary specialists, and find what aspects of complementary therapy are supportive for you personally.

COUNSELLING

Consulting a counsellor is not simply a question of being told how to cope with cancer and being led along a straightforward path which contains all the answers. It is often about admitting that you need help, and using a counsellor may be a means of finding out how you can help yourself. There is, amongst patients, a resistance to obtaining psychological support, which stems from a belief that people should be able to sort their problems out for themselves. Simply expressing your fears and anxieties may make it easier for you to cope with your feelings. A trouble shared is very often a trouble halved. After you have overcome your initial reluctance, it is possible to work through the feelings and take some solace from what might otherwise be a very painful situation.

Counselling may be necessary, not only to discuss the situation that has arisen and its implications, but also to view life more objectively, assess your own reaction to the situation and the contribution which this itself makes. It is not uncommon for families experiencing such intense emotions to vent them by expressing anger or resentment towards another individual – possibly a member of the family or a friend. There are no hard and fast rules as to who should be a counsellor. Cancer charities, and a large proportion of complementary medicine centres, will be able to advise, if not offer their own counsellor. A professional counsellor has probably had formal training over a period of months or years and will have experience of cancer sufferers and their families. However, a GP, or another partner in the same surgery who has experience in counselling and psychotherapy, may provide a preferable alternative for many individuals, as they can be approached more discreetly and anonymously.

Accepting that there is a problem and asking for help is more than half the battle. Once you can face the problem directly, you are in a position to do something about it. A counsellor is simply acting as a catalyst to expedite this process.

Sometimes, people who have experienced the death of a close friend or relative, or who have suffered from cancer themselves, subsequently find a sense of purpose in their lives by becoming counsellors and setting up support groups which make things that much easier for other people. Dr Vicky Clement-Jones, a doctor at St Bartholomew's Hospital in London, was one such person. Having had ovarian cancer, she felt there was a need for an organization such as BACUP (British Association of Cancer United Patients). This organization provides free telephone advice to cancer foundations and families. It is staffed by specially trained nurses who are able to give specific information about different cancer types and on services available locally. It now receives well over 100 calls a day from all over the UK. When BACUP was first established, many doctors were sceptical and some even opposed it, feeling it might undermine patients' confidence. But now most doctors realize how useful such a service can be, and some hospitals are trying to provide their own cancer information units for patients. There is now a free phoneline for people telephoning from outside London.

As well as individual counselling or psychotherapy, joining a self-help group may well be useful. Here a group of patients meet, usually with a group leader, to discuss their feelings. Many find this helpful, but a few dread going along. Our advice is not to be bullied by well-meaning relatives or friends to do anything you feel uncomfortable about. Information about such groups should be available at the hospital involved in your treatment – if not, telephone BACUP for details (*see Useful Information*).

There are also a number of smaller, more specific, societies, with interest in particular malignancies, which have been founded by the patients themselves or their relatives who have been victims of the disease, and have provided support which did not exist when they were faced with a similar situation. Groups have been established with a range of connections with cancer — for people with stomas, for some of the rarer cancers, for patients coming to terms with having had a mastectomy. If you are having difficulty adapting to a new situation, the likelihood is that you are not the first person in that position, and one of your 'predecessors' may well have established a group. Some useful addresses of such groups may be found in the Useful Information section at the end of this book.

RELAXATION

There are numerous forms of relaxation and meditation which can be used to help cancer patients and their families. Many people cope with periods of severe emotional stress by frenetic overactivity. They become absorbed in some alternative pastime in the hope that they can shut out their emotions until much of the pain has passed. Relaxation and meditation provide the means to a positive mental attitude. This is something which is always to be encouraged by those involved with conventional treatment of cancer, and those concerned with complementary therapy. Such a positive attitude makes treatment more tolerable, is likely to improve the patient's well-being, and logically should improve the individual's chance of being one of the 100,000 people whose malignancy spontaneously regresses.

There are some extreme views for which there is little supportive, scientific evidence. Laurence Le Shan believes that cancer can be cured by suppressing the 'cancer personality' – the many attributes which led to the person developing the cancer in the first place. Le Shan believes that 'the people most capable of recovery are those who can discover a new well-spring of hope and move on to a fresh sense of themselves, a true recognition of their worth as human beings'. This is perfectly acceptable if your malignancy is likely to be curable or you are amongst the small proportion of people who have a spontaneous remission. Unfortunately, for many patients, such an approach may well result in guilt on the part of the victim, or blame for their families for providing an environment in which cancer was able to develop. The diagnosis of cancer can carry with it enough feelings of blame and guilt under normal circumstances, without having to search for hidden psychological clues as to what caused it. There is a danger in suggesting that cancer is the result of stress, since modern life, for many reasons, is more likely to be stressful. People who smoke, eat unwisely and spend long periods in the sun are more likely to develop cancer than teetotal, non-smoking workaholics. With that proviso, it is nevertheless sensible to accept that cancer is an enormous challenge and that, in order to meet that challenge, it is appropriate to dissipate the effects of emotional stress through relaxation and meditation.

MEDITATION

Meditation is a state of freedom from thought, and in this respect is comparable to sleep. In the process, physical activity and, therefore, the body's metabolic rate, are decreased and it has a restoring quality which, for those who are able to meditate, is generally more versatile than sleep! Relaxation techniques are used increasingly by people in varying walks of life – not necessarily those with any form of illness. Relaxation and meditation are similar in many ways. The techniques may be different, but the ultimate goal is the same. In addition to individual therapists, who may be expensive, there are also books and tapes which provide instruction in both relaxation and meditation techniques. Many of these methods originated in the East and have been adapted to have particular relevance to patients 'with cancer. Transcendental Meditation was brought to the West by the Buddhists. There are a number of centres throughout Britain where you can learn the methods and spend periods at retreats with others.

In summary, these techniques can be self-taught (although they may be better taught by a therapist) and have both physical and mental benefits. They emphasize an approach to cancer in which the mind and spirit are as important as the body in responding to the disease. You must not have unrealistic expectations of what can be achieved, and any negative feelings of blame, guilt and anger, which these therapies enforce, are best avoided. As with any form of treatment for cancer, be it complementary or conventional, you must be the ultimate arbiter.

VISUALIZATION

There are two broad ways in which visualization can be used positively by cancer patients. In constructive visualization, the disease and its individual components are imagined as other forms, such as animals or inanimate objects. The patient's tumour may be given a name, and the therapy which he or she is having may be imagined in an analogous form. The choice is left very much to the individual, although the counsellor may help. One patient receiving monoclonal antibody therapy for ovarian cancer imagined the antibodies, which were labelled with radioactive isotope, as missiles which were helping her body's own resources. She imagined her white blood cells as goldfish which were 'Hoovering' up around her body. She saw the goldfish dressed in smart butler's uniforms pushing vacuum cleaners around inside her abdomen to suck up the cancer cells. This particular patient called her disease 'Fred'. She treated him as a friend who she had to keep at bay and, although she did not allow herself to become angry with Fred, she knew when enough was enough!

Another form of visualization is one used by the Chinese. In this exercise, described as bone breathing visualization, the patient sees the centre of the bones as responsible for the well-being of the entire body. Once in a comfortable, relaxed position, they are encouraged to imagine their breath entering the body and being taken up by each of the bones in turn as the breath circulates around the body. They concentrate on the legs initially, then the arms and hands followed by the spine and ultimately the skull. The exercise is repeated, breathing in gently and then breathing out through all the bones. In this approach, visualization is used as a means of facilitating relaxation.

HEALING

Healing is a process on which The Bristol Centre have placed great emphasis. It is patient-centred and quite distinct from cure. Cure is the term generally used for a successful medical treatment, and is seen as what the doctor hopes to effect for the patient. Healing, by contrast, is an inner process whereby a person becomes whole. It can take place at a physical level, as with a wound, but also at an emotional, psychological or spiritual level.

Like meditation, healing comes in many forms. Christian Science was founded at the end of the nineteenth century by Mary Baker Eddy and is based on the theory that illness can be overcome by faith and prayer. Spiritualism also had its origins in the nineteenth century with the establishment of a number of groups. It has the happy distinction of believing that healing is favourable to atheists as well as believers. The laying on of hands, which involves the healer passing his or her hands up and down the body, is a service offered by various religious organizations. It has been known to ease out pain. Descriptions of hand healing go back as far as the seventeenth century. Such a gift is thought to be possessed by very few people.

The Humanist Association works from a set of beliefs and moral ideals outside religious doctrines. Healing is available via a number of sources: a healer may be visited in his own centre, he may be contacted by post and may even visit individuals in their own homes when they are seriously ill. Whatever the means, the type of healing or the individual who administers it, it is essentially an adjunct to conventional therapy which should not be promising cures, but offering a means of maximizing the individual's chances.

The Simonton Technique was devised by Stephanie Simonton, the author of a book entitled *The Healing Family* (Bantam, 1984). It is based around a family game plan in which images of normal everyday life can be visualized through meditation and relaxation in order to promote healing and recovery. Stephanie Simonton, along with her husband, also wrote *Getting Well Again* (Bantam, 1980), a book which is aimed at people with cancer. It may be useful reading for many patients who find the method of visualizing images a fruitful one.

Although curing and healing are different, they are intertwined. Healing is part of the concept of the patient as a whole – a holistic approach – and it acknowledges the patient's crucial role in the outcome of the disease. Healing encourages patient involvement and more informed choice in the whole of your management. If you feel you would like to understand more about healing there are many books on the subject.

HYPNOTHERAPY

Hypnotherapy is closely related to the use of imagery and relaxation – all are part of voluntary control of internal states of consciousness. It has been widely used for cancer patients and involves three basic strategies – stress reduction, wellness enhancement and 'direct immunotherapy'. Stress reduction focuses on identifying stressful situations in a patient's life, and desensitizing the patient to them, to enhance coping skills. Wellness-enhancement involves creating a feeling of well-being, and improving mental health by a general focus on improving quality of life and quality of relationships. 'Direct immunotherapy' (not to be confused with its parallel in conventional medicine) involves stimulating the immune system by imagery.

The most well-known use of hypnotherapy in cancer patients is as a mechanism for suppressing the 'passive cancer personality'. This is a particular configuration of personality that is said to make the patient more prone to develop cancer and then, having developed it, makes them more prone to succumb. The objective evidence to support the existence of a cancer personality is conflicting. There is a suggestion that women who have a more positive approach, the fighting spirit, do better when treated for breast cancer. This may simply be that their more positive approach enables them to tolerate treatment and hence complete the course; improving their outlook in that way.

The passive cancer personality is said to be characterized by denial and repression, along with strong internalized control. Hypnotherapy can be used to overcome this mind-set and is, therefore, seen as a means of improving the outcome for the individual.

HOMOEOPATHY

Homoeopathy is the science of treating a condition by the administration, usually in miniscule doses, of drugs which produce symptoms in a healthy person similar to the disease being treated. This system was founded by Samuel Hahnemann of Leipzig at the end of the eighteenth century. The assumption that 'like cures like' is contrary to any of the foundations of orthodox medicine. Homoeopathy has been popular with the Royal Family throughout this century, and there are numerous stories which support it. Prince Charles made a famous speech to the British Medical Association in 1983 in which he encouraged doctors to be more broad-minded about alternative (complementary) medicines. In homoeopathy, small amounts of various drugs are given in an extremely dilute 'potentized' form. Consequently, it is without side-effects. This form of complementary medicine has also become more widely available, with an increasing number of medically qualified homoeopathic physicians. Non-medically qualified practitioners also exist and can be contacted through the Society of Homoeopaths. Two points must be kept in mind:

1) *no homoeopath should guarantee a cure unreservedly.*

2) *no homoeopath should demand that conventional treatment is abandoned.*

Most sympathetic homoeopaths will be happy to treat patients with homoeopathic medicine alongside their conventional treatments. In this way, homoeopathy can provide a useful supportive measure to those who find their symptoms are not relieved by conventional treatment, even though they believe it may be the best option for their cancer.

HERBAL MEDICINE

Much of modern pharmacology is based on the use of herbs. The vinca alkaloids are an important part of the treatment of many cancers, and their source is the Madagascan periwinkle. Doxorubicin (Adriamycin) was first extracted from a fungus found on the Adriatic coast, and one of the newest recruits to the armamentarium, Taxol™, is derived from the bark of a rare type of yew tree. Herbalism is both an art and a science, and forms part of the holistic approach to cancer. The herbalist uses particular groups of herbs. Some may detoxify by working on the liver, others purify the lymphatic system, and there are herbs which claim to block the growth of cancer cells. A good herbalist, working alongside a doctor, may be able to help patients adapt to their situation.

One sub-group of herbalism is the flower remedies of Dr Edward Bach, who worked in the early part of this century on preparing 38 remedies from wild flowers. He was a pathologist and bacteriologist who switched to homoeopathy at the turn of the century. He believed the negative emotions in cancer patients needed to be treated and, by holding his hand over a plant, he was able to experience the properties of that plant and thereby use it to treat the individual's emotions appropriately. The therapy is completely safe and without side-effects.

DIETARY TREATMENTS

The key to any diet is to adopt a sensible, balanced, healthy approach. This cannot be said of many of the diets currently recommended. Diet is a form of control whereby patients can become passive in relation to their disease. The Bristol Diet, which was followed more religiously when The Bristol Cancer Centre was initially established, involves three months of intensive strict vegan diet in which 90 per cent of the food must be raw, with the idea of cleansing the body of cancer. Subsequently, the diet has relaxed, without so much deprivation, and at this point it is intended to maintain the patient's remission.

There is also a Bristol Diet recommended to prevent cancer. The obvious problem with anything purporting such results is that, since one in three of us is likely to develop this disease, it is not unlikely that one in three individuals adhering to the diet will feel that they have failed in spite of having made a Herculean effort. There are a number of aspects of the Bristol Diet, and many like it recommended at different centres throughout the world, which are worrying to orthodox physicians. The word 'poisons' is frequently used for substances which many people take unavoidably throughout the course of their normal lives, such as fluoride. 'Poison' is a dangerous emotive word which, for many people with cancer, conjures up guilt and blame, both of which are negative and destructive emotions at a time when the individual has quite enough to contend with.

Vitamin supplements are also encouraged alongside the diet. If the diet is sensible and well-balanced, a vitamin supplement – the man-made equivalent of something which occurs naturally – should not be necessary for a normal healthy life. Eating 90 per cent raw food for three months, apart from being a severe deprivation for many people, is likely to be impractical. Housebound elderly people may well find it difficult to prepare their own food, and cannot expect 'Meals on Wheels' to serve up such diets on a regular basis! It seems logical that a person facing his or her biggest battle yet should feel positive and hopeful. Many of the diets recommended will make individuals feel deprived, and very often they will suffer gastro-intestinal symptoms which outweigh those caused by their disease.

Many alternative treatments acknowledge that diet is an essential part of the treatment of cancer, and some of the more extreme suggest that it is the major part of a person's lifestyle which has to change. Dr Max Gerson founded the Gerson Clinic at La Gloria Hospital in Tijuana , Mexico. His theory purports that cancer is a generalized chronic degenerative disease which is a symptom of a chronically damaged body. The Gerson therapy is based on a detoxification process whereby the body is treated with minerals and organic foods, having been purged by a strict vegan diet, coffee enemas and large quantities of fresh fruit juice. This is an expensive, monotonous, intensive and time-consuming process. An individual who has been through the mill in this way may well feel that they have not only taken full control of their body, but they have made a very active gesture in attempting to alter the course of their disease. But the evidence that such treatments effectively control tumour growth is slim. However, drastically changing your lifestyle may well be an effective means of coping with the psychological effects of the disease, even if it does not deal with the biological process of your cancer.

The ability of the cell to protect against the cancer-causing effects of environmental hazards such as chemicals and radiation is related to its oxidant state. Factors within the cell, which include micronutrients and vitamins, act as antioxidants to protect the cell against raised levels of free radicals, which may damage the cell. Vitamins C, E and A all have antioxidant activity. Superoxide dismutase is one of a number of naturally occurring antioxidant enzymes which undoubtedly have a role in the body. As they work at a cellular level, it is not certain yet whether they are effective when given as therapy for the treatment of established cancer, but they probably have a role in its prevention.

Carcinogens are substances which can cause, or play a part in, the development of cancer. They are usually found in the environment and may be natural or man-made. They have usually been identified from an association between exposure to, or consumption of, a particular substance which is then subsequently associated with an increased risk of certain types of cancer. Salt-cured, salt-pickled and smoked foods are undoubtedly associated with an increased incidence of stomach and oesophageal cancer, and are thought to explain the high incidence of these cancers seen in China, Japan and Iceland. Alcohol is also associated with a greater risk of some cancers, particularly those of the head and neck, and oesophagus. The combination of excessive alcohol and cigarettes leads to an even greater risk of these same cancers.

So what should you really do about diet if you have cancer? The main thing is to eat healthy, balanced meals of foods you enjoy. Make sure there is plenty of roughage in the form of fibre, as in brown bread and bran contained in cereals. This will avoid intestinal problems. Eat plenty of fresh fruit and lightly cooked vegetables. This should provide all the vitamins you need without resorting to artificial medication. Proponents of large doses of vitamins conveniently forget that the body just passes the excess out in the urine fairly smartly. Reduce your fat intake; avoid fried foods. Experiment with different diets – you might well like vegetarian food which is delicious and easy to digest. But above all, eat what you like and feel comfortable with, rather than adhering to some rigid schedule based on any scientific-sounding mumbo jumbo. Some cancer patients will have their diet restricted by the treatment, the surgery which they have had or the effects of their tumour. During radiotherapy to the abdomen or pelvis you are likely to develop a degree of diarrhoea. This is prevented or limited by a low-residue diet, and you will probably be given a diet listing foods to avoid – those high in fibre – and those to replace them with. This is only relevant during your radiotherapy, and sometimes for a few months afterwards. If you have a colostomy, you may be given dietary advice if much of your bowel has been removed, as this will make your stools more watery – again a low-residue diet will be advised. Similarly, patients at risk of bowel obstruction will be given advice about how to decrease this risk by eating a softer, more refined diet, and avoiding more indigestible food.

As to a diet for healthy cancer patients who simply want to improve their chances, there is very little concrete evidence to base suggestions on. There are no randomized, controlled clinical trials of therapeutic diets showing whether they may contribute to quality of life or improving prognosis. Various approaches have been tried by nutritionists, and these include calorie restriction, or under-feeding, or restriction of specific macronutrients (protein, fat and carbohydrate) or micronutrients (vitamins and trace elements). There is important evidence in favour of both sides of this argument, but there is nothing to suggest that restriction itself will help with the treatment of cancer. As far as the immune system is concerned, a balanced diet along the lines outlined below is sound advice.

WHAT TO EAT

- *Eat what you like when you want to.*

- *If you have lost weight, eat small meals frequently rather than getting stuck into a single large meal every day. Soups are often delicious and easy to take.*

- *Eat plenty of fibre – brown bread, bran, cereals.*

- *Eat lots of fresh fruit.*

- *Do not overcook vegetables – they will taste better, and the vitamins will not be destroyed.*

- *Avoid too much fat – have boiled or baked potatoes instead of chips.*

- *Reduce your red meat intake – it's more difficult to digest – and by all means stimulate the appetite with a glass of sherry or an appetizer.*

CONCLUSION

If becoming completely absorbed by complementary therapy makes you feel that life is worth while, then why not? However, you should think of it not as an alternative to conventional medicine but as an optional extra. You must weigh up the odds yourself. If complementary therapy causes physical symptoms and makes you feel depressed and isolated, then avoid it. If you are receiving highly intensive orthodox treatment, experiencing unpleasant side-effects, and finding it emotionally stressful, then complementary treatment of some sort may give you much needed encouragement.

The saying 'where there's life there's hope' is never more true than for cancer patients. Much of the unpleasant intensive treatment involved in pursuing a cure, or a further remission from cancer, is only possible because the individual still has hope. If using complementary therapy makes you feel more hopeful, then it may be of great benefit. Some of the successes of complementary therapy appear to be almost miracle cures, which cannot be explained on any logical scientific basis. For many people, such stories provide a ray of light at the end of the tunnel, and for this reason, if for no other, orthodox practitioners should encourage complementary therapy alongside conventional medicine.

There is a wide range of similar forms of complementary therapy which have been devised by various individuals from both conventional and self-taught backgrounds. There are many sources of information. Please beware of any which suggest stopping conventional therapy or using one type of complementary therapy but no other.

CHAPTER TEN

After Treatment

I t may be hard to imagine that life goes on after cancer. Many people undergo treatment while they are still experiencing the initial shock of diagnosis. When this is over, their attempt to return to a normal life is often an uphill struggle. For most patients and their families the experience of cancer, whatever its outcome, will change their lives for ever. Their values may be realigned, their whole perspective will be changed and life itself often takes on a much more intense focus. It is important in this process that patient and family do not become victims. Although at first it may be hard to view anything with a long-term perspective, restoration to a full emotional life is every bit as important as successful therapy (*see Figure 10.1*). If the price of cure is isolation and fear, nobody will benefit.

Having completed your course of therapy, you may attend the first follow-up clinic expecting to be told that you have been cured. Unfortunately, cancer is not like that. By the time it has been discovered, there are usually over a billion cancer cells in the body. The vast majority of these cells will have disappeared during treatment, but present-day screening techniques mean that we cannot detect even as many as ten thousand cells accurately. As a result, any doctor who tells a patient, as little as one month after treatment, that they have been cured, is being inappropriately optimistic. It may be very likely that they have been cured, but a definitive statement is not possible at this stage.

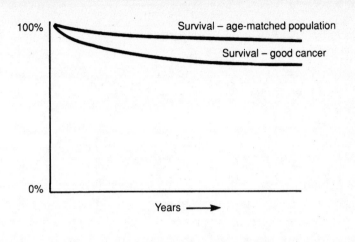

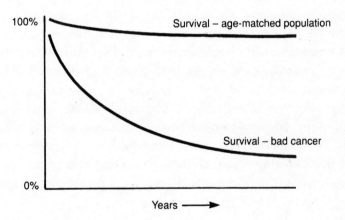

Figure 10.1 *Survival curves of 'good' and 'bad' cancers.*

FOLLOW-UP

Follow-up clinics are useful for both you and your doctor. It may take some time to cease dreading these occasions, but as the gaps between clinics increase, reassurance comes. The clinic is there as a safety net to which you can return if your symptoms recur, or fears about the disease become overwhelming. The most important factor your doctor can learn from your clinic is how you are feeling. Blood tests, X-rays and other investigations may be part of monitoring, but a very well patient with no symptoms is unlikely to have a recurrence. On the other hand, someone who is depressed or has become obsessed with their disease and is unable to return to a normal life, needs encouragement and reassurance.

The follow-up visit usually begins with a discussion about any symptoms. The doctor will then examine you and arrange for any necessary tests to be carried out. As we learn more about cancer it is becoming apparent that fewer tests, rather than more, are indicated. In the vast majority of tumours, we do not have reliable ways of following patients up and discussing whether they have relapsed or whether they have developed microscopic disease away from the site of the original tumour. In those cancers where any recurrence or spread of the disease is likely to respond well to treatment, and where there are sensitive tests which can detect relapsed disease, tests are likely to be done to ensure that any problems are detected at an early stage. In these malignancies, blood tests, X-rays and scans are important and will be a regular part of the patient's review. In many situations, tests will not be carried out unless there are obvious worrying symptoms. You should not feel that you are being neglected simply because an investigation is not performed. Ideally, most patients would hope to reach a point where visits are necessary only once or twice a year, and it may be that in future years some of this follow-up process will be performed by paramedical staff and not doctors, or perhaps your GP.

GETTING BACK TO WORK

The diagnosis of cancer is likely to be followed by an operation, or at least a biopsy, then radiotherapy and or chemotherapy. It may well be three or four months before you have completed your treatment, and perhaps another few months before you feel well enough to return to work, although some people manage to work through their radiotherapy or chemotherapy, only missing that part of the day taken up by treatment, or a few days for short admissions to receive drugs.

Your GP or family doctor can advise about any benefits or financial support to which you may be entitled.

Once employers are aware of the reasons for your absence, they may have their own ideas about your subsequent ability to do your job. It is essential to enlist the support and help of your medical staff at this point. Any specific disability can be anticipated. If certain tasks associated with your job are impossible, it may be feasible to amend your job so that you can cope. However, there is no reason why most people cannot resume full employment exactly as before, once they have had a chance to regain their strength. Getting back to work is the most important factor in returning to a normal life, and much of your self-esteem is likely to depend on this. If you have any specific difficulties in relation to your job or employer, you should air these in the clinic. An explanatory letter from the doctor concerned will often do much to dispel any fears and misconceptions. It is not only patients with cancer who fear the disease; its taboos extend to people close to that person. Irrational behaviour from family, friends and work colleagues is not unusual, and the only way this can be countered is to avoid mystery and replace it with understanding.

FINANCIAL PROBLEMS

These can be divided into short- and long-term problems. The latter include returning to full-time employment, the possibility of ultimate invalidity and the fear of having a surviving family inadequately cared for. All of us, whether in full health, young or old, with or without dependants should make a will. If this has not been done before the diagnosis of cancer, it should be undertaken as soon as possible thereafter. However uncomplicated the will, it is probably best to consult a solicitor when drawing it up so as to avoid misunderstandings between the beneficiaries. For most patients, unless the will is complex, the expense of a solicitor will not be very great. Not only will everyone be assured of the legalities, but a solicitor's advice on ways to minimize estate duty could save a lot of money.

As far as the short term is concerned, the financial support you receive during your treatment will vary from employer to employer. Most people are entitled to Government-funded sick pay and, if the period of illness continues, possibly sickness benefit or invalidity benefit as well. This is likely to fall short of your usual income, and most people will be keen to return to work as soon as possible. Many people find the idea of having a social worker allocated to them as somehow rather shameful, as if they are problem cases who can't cope, and they will not ask for these services until they are desperate. This is unfortunate, as social workers can often help out in the early stages and avoid any later crises. They are also able to advise about contributions from special funds for cancer patients and which sources to approach for expenses such as fares and accommodation, and for obtaining free prescriptions and attendance allowance where appropriate. The Cancer Relief Macmillan Fund in the UK has an annual budget of £1.5 million which is distributed to patients in need, particularly for helping getting to and from hospital for treatment and follow-up appointments, and for families to visit patients. For children with cancer, the Malcolm Sargent Fund serves a similar purpose.

If you need to be cared for at home at any point, your family may be entitled to an attendance allowance or a care allowance. You can get details of who to claim from and when and how to claim, most easily through a social worker. Patients with a colostomy, ileostomy or urostomy are all entitled to free prescriptions – not only for anything to do with their operation but for any other drugs or dressings they may need.

In the long term, you may find you are no longer able to pay your rent or insurance. If you can't go back to work, your mortgage payments will be subject to the same restrictions as anybody on sick pay or sickness benefit. As for life insurance, those who do not have to worry are those who are already adequately covered. If you are thinking about taking out new life insurance policies after treatment it is worth contacting the Association of British Insurers (*see Useful Information*) to ask for a list of insurers who look favourably on people who have recently had a diagnosis of cancer. It may well be possible to shop around to compare their rates, or alternatively wait for a period of one year, when rates may be more favourable still. Often insurers will reduce their rates as the disease-free interval increases, and it is worth keeping this in mind and enquiring regularly. Once again, information from your doctor and the nature of your diagnosis, stage of disease, and your likely prognosis will be essential to obtain insurance. The content of the letter should be discussed with you, but from the point of view of understanding your likely prognosis and whether the doctor feels you are a reasonable risk for life insurance.

Drawing up and making funeral arrangements is probably best discussed when it is least likely to be particularly relevant. A social worker may be a useful means of support and, if special funds are needed these can be obtained at the relevant time from a number of cancer charities. Alternatively, you may prefer to set aside a sum of money to take the burden from your family.

TALKING TO OTHERS

This is something that will happen from an early stage in your treatment. You will meet other patients in the chemotherapy clinic, whilst waiting for your radiotherapy and on the ward after surgery. They will be at varying stages with their disease and will have very differing stories of their experiences. This can sometimes be very confusing, and it may help to approach a specific support group. This could be a general one, such as BACUP (British Association of Cancer United Patients), or CancerLink; or, alternatively, a charity used to dealing with one particular type of cancer. Many of the bigger charities and organizations have a helpline that is manned at least part of the week, and may have regular local association meetings. They may publish pamphlets about particular illnesses which can provide information in greater clarity and detail than it is possible to glean from the doctor at the clinic. In addition, you can get support from the hospital treating you, with care continuing after your discharge from hospital and after the completion of your treatment. This supplements home visits from a district nurse, your practice nurse, or visits from other paramedical staff.

Many people who have recently been diagnosed as having cancer will feel angry and very frightened. By meeting others in a similar situation, particularly those who are further down the road with their disease, you can see how they cope. We are all different, however, and you must keep this in mind when comparing your own experiences with those of others. You should not feel a failure if your illness does not progress as well as someone else's. At times, the information you obtain from different sources can be conflicting, and it is then important to ask your specialist if you do not understand the conflicting information that you have received. He or she will then be able to explain the position more fully, and probably relieve much of your stress. If you are not happy about your management, and feel that you have not explored all the possible avenues, ask for a second opinion. This is, and always has been, readily available under the NHS. A sympathetic family doctor who understands what the options are in your area, and has contact with cancer specialists, will probably be able to help you at this point.

RECURRENT DISEASE

The ultimate fear of most patients is that their cancer will return. As time goes by, so the risk of recurrence decreases, and your follow-up visits to the clinic will become less frequent. Of course, the chances of recurrence depend on what type of cancer you have had, and how far it had spread when you were first treated. Some highly aggressive cancers will probably recur within two years of diagnosis if they are going to recur at all and, if you have been disease-free for five years, in most malignancies the likelihood is that you have been cured. On the other hand, there are diseases that respond to primary treatment, but many years later, sometimes decades, cells that have spread from the primary site begin to grow, causing problems again. Many cancers, possibly up to half, can still be cured at the time of diagnosis. These include those which are sensitive to hormone therapy, such as breast cancer and prostatic cancer, those which can be cured by chemotherapy (e.g. lymphomas and testicular tumours) or those where the only problem is a local recurrence, and further surgery or radiotherapy can control the disease without it spreading further.

Although some cancers cannot be cured, this may not, in fact, reduce the patient's life expectancy. Many patients live with their cancer for many years. It causes little in the way of symptoms, and they are quite often able to reach normal life expectancy. Other patients may have numerous recurrences of their malignancy, with the periods of remission between recurrences being of a reasonable length.

It is also important to maintain a balance between the length of time a patient is expected to survive and their quality of life. If someone is expected to live only a few months, even with treatment, and the treatment itself is likely to cause unpleasant side-effects, then the patient's quality of life – and personal dignity – will obviously suffer. For this reason, any decision about further treatment should take into consideration possible side-effects, the chances of good periods of remission, the number of clinic visits involved and the likely outcome. Since the implications for the patient are far greater than for the doctor, the doctor must be aware of the patient's priorities. One common misconception about further treatment is that it is unlimited. If radical radiotherapy has already been given, the normal tissue in that area will probably not be able to withstand any further dose without being irreparably damaged. Most tumours are sensitive to only a limited number of drugs, and once these have been exhausted, options become increasingly limited. Furthermore, both radiotherapy and chemotherapy are toxic to the bone marrow stem cells and, in patients who have already received intensive treatment, further treatment may result in prolonged bone marrow suppression. This means that the reproduction of white blood cells (which fight infection) and platelets (one of the factors involved in blood clotting) will be lowered, leaving the patient at greater risk of infection, spontaneous bruising and bleeding. As a result, patients may require frequent stays in hospital for antibiotics to treat or prevent infections, or transfusions of platelets if these are low. Bone marrow suppression is the most common problem which limits further treatment, but damage to the kidneys, the nerves (both those in the spinal cord and those supplying the limbs), the small intestine and lungs can all result from chemotherapy or radiotherapy. Radiotherapy essentially only damages the area which is treated, whereas chemotherapy, because it is given through a vein and circulates around the body, can damage any part of the body. Further treatment can cause as many problems to the patient as recurrence of the disease.

PAIN CONTROL

One of the great fears of any cancer patient is pain. Part of the taboo stems from a fear that their last few months will be spent in uncontrolled pain. In fact, virtually half the patients who die with cancer never experience pain at any point. Moreover, with increased understanding of cancer we can now anticipate the problem. By making frequent adjustments, the correct balance can be obtained between good pain-control 24 hours a day without causing unnecessary sleepiness and fatigue. It may be difficult to cure all cancers, but there can be no excuse for allowing people to suffer pain. Analgesics (painkillers) are given regularly so that pain never breaks through to the surface. Usually, patients will be given a painkiller such as paracetamol to start with and, if this is not enough, move on to a combination analgesic which contains paracetamol and another more powerful drug.

Anti-inflammatory tablets, such as aspirin, can also be used – these can be particularly helpful with bone pain. If they fail to control pain adequately, the opiate family of drugs are used. These are drugs derived from opium – an extract of the poppy. Dihydrocodeine, or codeine, are likely to be the first opiates used. Subsequently, morphine and diamorphine are the mainstay of pain control. Sadly, morphine is often thought of as a drug which is only given to patients when they are about to die. This is far from the truth. Indeed, some drugs such as slow-release morphine preparations (like MST) can be used by patients with severe pain for many years. As for opiates being addictive, there is little to support this theory unless they are injected directly into a vein. If the patient is experiencing pain, the opiates are likely to be badly needed, but they can be reduced fairly rapidly once the pain has resolved. It is only when patients have been on opiate drugs for more than a period of weeks that they cannot be withdrawn suddenly. It is also known that in patients in severe pain there are higher levels of naturally occurring receptors which mop up drugs such as morphine and diamorphine, and consequently such patients are not at risk of opiate addiction.

The fear of using opiate analgesia is not unique to patients, and there are some doctors who are reluctant to use such treatment. In fact, opiates are remarkably safe. Many of the problems experienced by drug abusers are the result of infections from unhygienic needles and syringes. One of the advantages which the opiates have over other groups of painkillers is that they are not only more powerful and effective painkillers but they carry with them a euphoriant effect which often helps by giving the patient a sense of well-being. Morphine is said to shorten patient's lives, but there are no observations to support this idea. Someone in severe pain, and persistently distressed, is more likely to have a rapid unhappy demise than a patient with good pain control who is able to lead a peaceful and calm life in his or her own surroundings.

Opiates only cause hallucinations if given in large doses, and they should not be withheld on the grounds that the patient is not sufficiently unwell or in pain to justify them. As long as they are started at a relatively low dose, they can be matched to the level of pain. Some individuals are particularly sensitive to opiates, and by starting at a low dose this can be detected. If undue drowsiness results, they are simply stopped.

How Painkillers Are Given

In patients who require quick-acting analgesics which vary widely from day to day, it may be best to switch from a tablet or syrup form, such as those available with opiate analgesics, to a small pump. A tiny needle is inserted just under the skin, and supplies a continuous infusion of the drug from a syringe fixed in a small battery-operated or clockwork pump. There is no real difference between morphine and diamorphine, apart from the actual dose required, although the latter is more soluble and is more likely to be used when given in infusions. This is ideal for patients who are nursed at home, since the patient or member of the family can be taught to site the fine needle under the skin themselves and make up the drug so that the syringe can be changed once a day. This form of pain control has really helped to make life much more tolerable. Occasionally, patients have such severe pain that the doses of opiates required are sufficient to impair their level of consciousness. In this situation, the drug can be administered directly into the fluid surrounding the spinal cord. A catheter is inserted by an anaesthetist in much the same way as an epidural catheter is used for women in labour. The cannula in the spine is held in place, and a small reservoir is attached outside. When the patient has particularly severe pain and needs an extra dose of the drug, he or she can press the reservoir, and a top-up dose will be delivered. This relatively novel form of pain control has been around for less than 10 years, and consequently has not been used widely outside the hospital setting. However, Macmillan Nurse teams with experience of giving pain control by means of a continuous infusion are becoming more widely accessible, and in forthcoming years we are likely to see an increasing switch to patients being cared for at home in their final months or weeks.

In addition to drugs, treatment itself can constitute a form of pain control. For bony pain and some painful skin lesions, a single dose of radiotherapy can alleviate the symptoms for a considerable time. Patients with widespread bony metastases may be admitted to hospital overnight and given a single dose of radiotherapy to the lower or upper half of the body. This is known as hemibody radiotherapy. With sedation and drugs to control sickness, the patient usually sleeps through the experience and many of the other side-effects. The main problems are nausea, perhaps vomiting and, where the lower half of the body is treated, a degree of diarrhoea and perhaps passing urine more frequently. For more localized secondary deposits, a short course of radiotherapy will often shrink the lesion causing the pain, and patients may find their regular analgesics can be tailed off. Similarly, chemotherapy, while not used for pain control, will automatically lessen pain if it reduces the painful site of the disease. The use of single doses to treat localized bony or other deposits is increasing, and you should not be alarmed if your doctor wants to help your pain by simply giving a single fraction of radiotherapy. The obvious advantage of this is that you do not have to make several visits to the hospital. We also know from trials involving large numbers of patients, that there is no advantage, in terms of pain relief or the period of time for which the pain is controlled, from giving more than one fraction.

CONTROLLING PAIN

- *Simple painkillers – aspirin, paracetamol.*

- *More potent analgesics – co-dydramol, co-proxamol, co-codamol, dihydrocodeine, distalgesic.*

- *Anti-inflammatory drugs – indomethacin, naproxen.*

- *Synthetic morphine-like drugs – Palfium (dextromoramide), Diconal (dipipanone), Fortral (pentazocine).*

- *Morphine and diamorphine given by mouth or by injection.*

- *Many drugs are made by several manufacturers and have different brand names, which adds to confusion – your doctor can advise.*

- *Whichever drugs are used, remember, you get no medals for being able to withstand pain.*

- *Your doctor (GP or hospital) can advise about how best to time pain-control medicine.*

DYING AND BEREAVEMENT

Once death has been accepted as inevitable, there has to be a change of approach by the doctors and nurses in relation to care and communication. This transition is often difficult to make within the hospital environment, as the staff have to look after potentially curable patients simultaneously. Consequently, there is a tendency for dying patients to be placed in a side ward and visited by the staff when necessary, but not spontaneously. Sixty per cent of the population in Great Britain die in hospital, and the figure is even higher in the United States. Sadly, it has increased in the past two decades, in spite of increasing awareness of continuing care and the possibility of being nursed at home.

THE HOSPICE MOVEMENT

The first form of care for the dying, which we now take for granted, was seen in the Middle Ages. At that time, hospices were run by religious organizations. In the nineteenth century, Mary Aikenhead opened the first modern hospice in Dublin. She founded the Irish Sisters of Charity, and one of their tasks was to care for the dying. From her experiences she decided that a nursing home was needed for dying patients which was quieter and smaller than a hospital for the acutely ill. She used her own house initially, and adopted the name of the resting places in the Holy Land – 'hospice'. At the beginning of the twentieth century, the Sisters opened St Joseph's Hospice in Hackney, London. Subsequently, two further hospices were founded in London, and in 1899 an order of Dominican Nuns had founded the first hospice in New York City.

Since that time there has been a great expansion in continuing care, and Britain now leads the world in terms of provision both for people dying in hospices and for those who wish to die at home. Although most of the earlier hospices were founded by religious orders, many NHS hospices have no particular denomination or leaning.

There are a number of advantages to hospice care. Some of these are for the relatives who may be exhausted or anxious, or trying hard to hold down full-time employment. Many dying patients live alone and are too weak to cope. They may require a specific medication or treatment which cannot easily be given at home. Many cancer patients are old and may not have relatives nearby. In addition, brave families who are doing their best to cope may benefit from short periods of respite care to allow them to recuperate. If there are particular complications of the patient's illness that are better cared for in the hospice and the family would like to be near the dying patient, it is usually possible to arrange for relatives to stay. In comparison with a busy ward, even one which has predominantly cancer patients, a hospice is likely to be more peaceful. The staff may not wear a nursing uniform, the wards are likely to be smaller and more home-like, and in most cases will have been designed with greater privacy for the patient and relatives. The staff will be particularly skilled in relieving symptoms associated with terminal illness, and will probably have broader experience and a wider range of possible ways of managing pain. Away from the hubbub of a busy ward within a hospital, the opportunity to receive counselling, talk to medical and nursing staff and spend time with relatives is more readily available. For many patients, particularly those with no close family, it is a much warmer and more positive place to be. The patients themselves are the *raison d'être* for the hospice, whereas on a mixed ward which has many patients still undergoing active treatment they may feel more like outsiders.

DYING AT HOME

More than 40,000 people die at home in Britain each year. A high proportion of these do not need any particular support. However, there is a significant minority who, without the support of the continuing care team, would need admission to an institution. After a survey instigated by the Marie Curie Foundation in the early 1950s, the needs of cancer patients and their relatives for adequate support were highlighted. In 1958, a day and night nursing service was introduced. Sadly, the availability of such services varies widely from region to region and, with the current financial constraints on the NHS, many have been reduced. In 1973 a nurse and doctor from St Joseph's Hospice began to visit dying patients at home. At that time the GPs were responsible for home support with the aid of district nurses. In 1975 St Joseph's Hospice established a service called Macmillan Nurses, which in its first three years cared for 1,000 patients dying from cancer. Many of these were able to spend most of their remaining weeks at home. This has led to the current situation, where more than 60 per cent of St Joseph's dying patients are at home. The lynchpins of this type of home-care team are the nurses. The number of visits they make vary but, where necessary, patients are visited up to eight times daily. In addition, there are doctors, social workers and physiotherapists available, all of whom contribute to keeping the patients at home for as long as possible. Such continuing care at home will vary geographically, and is likely to be better where the hospice is nearby. The hospital specialist, GP and social worker should all be able to inform the patient and family about the services available, and a determined family who feel strongly that the patient should be able to die at home should express this wish as early as possible. The advantages of dying at home are evident. The patient is in familiar surroundings, he or she has a chance to spend time with relatives, and is able to maintain both dignity and individuality. He or she is not lost in the anonymity of dying as a hospital or hospice in-patient, and the bereavement process is likely to be kinder.

If the final stage of the patient's illness is relatively long, it is worth exploring the possibility of installing gadgets and appliances to improve the quality of life and leave the family more independent. Cancer is an emotive disease which attracts more money for charity than any other. Consequently, a well-informed social worker will be able to direct the family to a number of different sources for grants to help with appliances, fares and numerous other items of expenditure which might not otherwise be manageable. This is likely to vary from country to country. Nevertheless, some form of continuing care facility will be available for most of us in the West, and hospices or their equivalent, along with Macmillan teams or equivalent, are gradually being established in some of the developing countries. Whether they are State-funded, run by the Church or organizations such as the Marie Curie Foundation. For those relatives or patients who realize they may be approaching the terminal phase of their illness, it is important to find out what is available in your geographical area and how access can be obtained.

BEREAVEMENT

Whenever someone dies, from whatever cause, their friends and relatives go through the process of bereavement. How long it will last and how severe the grief will depend on the closeness to the person who has died and their ability to cope with their own reactions. Time is a great healer in this respect. Many events resulting in disappointment are difficult to take at first. Even failing your driving test, not getting a job after an interview or failing an exam at school may fill you with despondency and gloom. A few years later these events are forgotten. In the same way, the process of bereavement allows you to adapt to the fact that a loved one will no longer be there and life will have to change to meet the new circumstances. However long the terminal phase of the illness, there will be a reaction of grief, although a long illness may provide an opportunity for many of the stages of bereavement to be experienced by patient and family simultaneously, prior to the patient's actual death. The one stage which almost invariably does not occur before death is acceptance.

The commonest emotion experienced by all of us will be grief. This may be preceded by short periods of shock and numbness when it is difficult to accept or fully absorb the implications. Subsequently, we are likely to feel desperate and sad, with a feeling of futility about life. We may retreat into ourselves with apathy, which is expressed in both mental and physical symptoms, withdrawing generally from society. Some people may be very agitated and restless, with no appetite and unable to sleep, and this itself may be coupled with feelings of self-doubt and guilt about the death of the loved one. They may find elaborate ways of blaming themselves for what has happened, or feel guilty about the way they behaved towards the dying person. Along with feelings of self-reproach, they may feel that others involved in caring for their loved one during the final illness are to blame.

Although we are all very different in our reactions, some components of grief are fairly predictable. It often helps to understand that we are not alone in our feelings. One problem that arises time and time again is the wish to have had a better relationship with the person who has died. If only we had done those things they wanted to do, gone on that holiday, bought that caravan, been less critical of their quirks. These feelings may take some months to disappear.

Sometimes we may deny that death has actually occurred. We may talk about things as though they were alive, and even make plans as if nothing had happened. Until death is accepted, it is difficult to reconcile the situation so that normal life can be resumed.

Severe grief reactions are usually considered as those which are particularly long. There is no accepted normal period of mourning. Somewhere between six months and a year is the usual time, the period being longer where the relationship was longer. Periods of grief may be suppressed for some time, only to return on specific occasions such as birthday, anniversary or the anniversary of the death itself. People who have experienced frequent losses may develop blunted responses. This was seen during the last two world wars. This blunting also occurs in children who have lost a parent. They are able to subdue their grief and, as a result deny a need for affection. This may interfere with their emotional development, and can sometimes cause problems in later life.

Those who lose people with cancer may experience an extreme fear of the disease – a reaction that may be even more likely if attempts have been made to avoid mentioning the disease and its effects. The development of symptoms similar to those suffered by the patient may also be a form of mourning. Consciously or unconsciously, the mourner may be taking on their characterization in an attempt to keep their memory alive. Severe bereavement reactions are not predictable. They appear to be more common in women, particularly those who are young or middle-aged when widowed, or those who have lost children. Whatever the mechanisms, the complexities and the period of mourning, it is an inevitable part of the loss associated with bereavement. It is a natural process, and only if it impairs the ability to return to normal life after a period should it be considered as abnormal. Whatever the reaction, it may be helped by professional support or perhaps a support group with people who have endured a similar experience. Having worked through the emotions provoked by bereavement, most of us can accept these emotions and find a balance where we can adjust to a new life with those left behind.

CASE HISTORY

Barbara was diagnosed with breast cancer at the age of 58. Two years later she developed pain in her spine, and it was found that the disease had spread. She was given the drug tamoxifen, and initially both her pain and the spread of the disease improved. Nine months later the pain had returned and she was switched to an alternative hormone therapy (Provera – a progestogen). This had only a short-lived response and thereafter she was given a course of chemotherapy. Over the next two years she continued to get better for periods and then deteriorate for a while, and she was given short courses of mild chemotherapy or radiotherapy to particularly troublesome areas when her symptoms became too severe.

She then developed severe pains in her left hip, and over a short period a fracture of her left hip bone became apparent. By this time her blood count was low as a result of her extensive radiotherapy and chemotherapy, and it was also suspected that the cancer was affecting her bone marrow. As a result, insufficient white blood cells, which fight infection, were being produced. Her bone abnormalities on the X-ray were now so widespread that even if the left hip were repaired it was likely that her spine would be the next problem. Barbara had already received a high dose of radiotherapy to her lower spine and had exhausted the range of drugs available, so there was little left to be offered in the way of conventional therapy.

Her left hip was operated on, fusing the thigh bone to the

pelvis, so that she could be transferred between the bed and chair without pain. By this time she was being nursed on a special bed (a Clinitron) which consists of a series of beads which float on a cushion of air. This enables the patient to be turned with minimal effort by the nurses and without discomfort for the patient. Having recovered from her hip operation, it was possible to organize the bed at home, with the local authority paying for the very high cost of hiring it. Barbara was transferred home with maximum support from the continuing care team, the district nurse, her family and with a bed on the same floor as the bathroom. She was nursed at home successfully for some weeks until she died, in the place and with the dignity which she had wanted.

CHAPTER ELEVEN

Controversies in Cancer

There is no doubt that cancer is an emotive disease capable of attracting publicity. It therefore comes as no surprise that scandals about the management of cancer make the headlines with monotonous regularity. On both sides of the Atlantic and the Channel we hear of patients being entered into unethical trials, receiving the wrong dose of radiation or simply that the results of large trials which have altered the management of a disease will not withstand close scrutiny.

As most of us are touched by cancer in some way, either personally or through a close relative or friend, many people are affected by these sensational news items, and may be sent into a panic unnecessarily. Here we attempt to look at some of these problems and, by explaining them, we hope to allay some of the fear and anxiety.

ACCESS TO CARE

This problem exists the world over. Even where the resources are spent on health care, not everybody will be covered, and where a comprehensive system is provided, such as in the UK, there are still ways in which individuals fall through the net. Having bought this book, you have selected yourself as informed and interested in the management of your, your relative's or friend's cancer. There will always be those who do not wish to be informed, or whose fear and misunderstanding of the disease lead them to ignore symptoms and signs which might enable an earlier diagnosis to be made. At this level access to care is based on education and information and not the health care system.

Then there is the geographical limit on access. If you live in a remote part of a country, some distance from the nearest cancer centre, your family physician or general practitioner may be more reluctant to refer you. If the journey is likely to be difficult, you may not seek help until later. Even having sought help you may find that your nearest hospital does not have the services of an oncologist and that, in your area, certain cancers are not managed by oncologists but by general physicians. Historically, this has often been true of lung cancer where the disease is perceived, with some justification, to have such a poor outlook that referral is not justified. Equally, where resources such as radiotherapy machine time are limited, the palliation of advanced lung cancer may be seen as a low priority as it improves quality of life but has no hope of cure. This limitation is not simply geographical, it is resource-related and will vary widely between countries.

RADIOTHERAPY

We will start with radiotherapy as it is one aspect of management of the cancer patient over which many patients feel they have no control. X-rays cannot be seen and yet they burn you and may cause serious side-effects. Although this isn't so different from lying on a hot beach under ultraviolet irradiation, most people feel they can exert some control over the latter situation. By contrast, with radiotherapy, you have to give up control and allow your doctor and then the radiographers and physicists to take the responsibility for giving the correct dose to the correct part of your body.

There have been scandals about under- and overtreatment of patients with radiotherapy. Overtreatment has occurred when a machine has been incorrectly calibrated and the mistake not picked up by staff at a later stage. Calibration is the careful calculation and testing of the dose of X-irradiation being delivered by a machine in a particular period of time. It is a technical process which, to avoid errors, must be performed regularly. In many cases this is only out by a few per cent, and the dose received by the patient is still within the range which might be given by radiotherapists practising in Europe and North America. Where the dose is higher than this it may be of some concern, particularly if it was delivered to a part of the body where the normal tissue is particularly sensitive to the effects of radiation. Often it will be picked up early on in treatment by the doctors or radiographers, as the patient will have a more marked radiation reaction than usual. Also, the machine calibration should be checked by more than one individual, and so a mistake at this point should be spotted by other physicists. As the management of cancer improves, the machines which deliver radiation improve in their sophistication, and the use of machines with sources – such as the cobalt machine where mistakes have previously arisen – should decrease. These accidents should become a thing of the past. The level of quality control is improving all the time.

Just as overdosage has occurred, so has underdosage. As the error is the result of incorrect calibration, the dose is just as likely to be too low as too high. Again, the level of variation in most cases could be within the limits of normal practice in different centres and between different specialists.

In the UK the Royal College of Radiologists, the representative body of Clinical Oncologists or Radiotherapists, undertook a survey of consultants and asked them how they would manage five different clinical problems. The majority responded, and the most surprising finding in the study was the enormous variation in the radiotherapy schedules which were used. These may reflect a number of factors: the centre where the individual concerned practised (if there was restricted machine-time available, shorter courses of radiotherapy involving larger doses per fraction may have to be used); the centre where they trained (doctors tend to use schedules with which they are familiar and have experience of the side-effects or late-effects); the distance the patient may have to travel; the need for a good cosmetic result; and whether the course is palliative or likely to be curative.

This variation may be particularly marked in the UK for a number of reasons. We allocate fewer resources to health care generally, and the management of cancer has in the past been a particularly bad example of this problem, with small numbers of specialists in the field, and a geographical sparsity of treatment centres outside the major cities. In the US, where you have a true free market in cancer care, there are likely to be more linear accelerators in a middle-class affluent town serving a population of a million people than there are in the whole of north London serving six times that population. Yet, on a national basis, London is relatively well provided for.

IMPORTANT POINTS ABOUT RADIOTHERAPY SCHEDULES

- *Small frequent fractions – tend to result in fewer long-term side-effects and better cosmetic results.*

- *Infrequent large fractions – may be suitable for pain control where disease has spread, distances to be travelled are longer or the patient is unwell.*

- *Slight overdosage or underdosage (up to 15 per cent) is likely to fall within the 'norms' of treatment variation between different centres and specialists.*

CLINICAL TRIALS

Much of what we do in cancer therapy is not always the best-accepted therapy. Indeed, in many instances there are no absolute right answers, and a number of alternatives could be employed by different oncologists. In order to improve on the current management of patients for future generations, we require evidence from clinical trials. The most important of these are known as Phase III trials, in which patients are randomized between one treatment option and another. Medicine is a rather patriarchal specialty, and patients are quite used to being told what treatment they need by their doctor, and then receiving it. For many patients it is difficult to accept that their doctor does not have all the answers, and in order to find these answers they need to be entered into a clinical trial. Many patients feel that they are being used as guinea pigs, and are not happy to be entered into trials. Not only is it confusing, but you may also have a preconception about which type of treatment you should receive, and find you have a 50 per cent chance of receiving this and then a 50 per cent chance of receiving something different. Yet, without Phase III trials we will not be able to answer the questions as to which is the better treatment. And where the difference between two treatments is only small, large numbers of patients need to be recruited to the trials in order to show that difference.

At the same time that these important issues need to be addressed, we are entering an era where the patient is regarded as a client or consumer, and their treatment should involve informed choice. Although this may cut across the needs to undertake clinical trials, in many centres, where doctors do not feel they have the time and resources to put their patients into trials, it may solve the problem of being uncertain as to which is the best course of action. When patients have all the available evidence in front of them, and this information is not confusing or misleading, they may be able to make a decision. Knowing all the pitfalls and advantages of each different course of action, patient-informed choice may lead to better doctor – patient relations and happier 'clients'.

PATIENT-INFORMED CHOICE

The concept of patient-informed choice originated in the United States in the 1970s with Dr John Wennberg. Since that time it has been taken up internationally and has a particular role in cancer treatment, where often there are no clear answers about their management. This is especially relevant in the treatment of breast cancer where the choices are legion and the benefits and disadvantages rather blurred. One way round this problem is to give patients material which explains the various options, what is entailed and how soft or hard the evidence is in favour of or against these options. The patient is then given the opportunity to decide which path to follow. This is at a relatively early stage and is still being carefully evaluated by those centres involved. Many patients want to be able to relinquish responsibility to their doctor and do not want to make the choice themselves. For others, they may believe they want this 'control' but find the emotional and psychological burden too great. The informed choice can be made through a number of different media – in the United States interactive videos have been developed and, if successful, these are likely to become more widely available in Europe over the forthcoming years. However, reading material, flow diagrams, tapes, videos and the opportunity to speak with medical and paramedical staff may prove as useful for many patients.

It is important to note that, for patient-informed choice to work well, it requires people to take time with the patient in ensuring that they fully understand all the options available. Counselling the patient, in helping them make this decision, is important as many patients find the responsibility very stressful. It is also important to evaluate any work being undertaken. This is a relatively new area, and there are obviously dangers as well as advantages in involving patients this closely in their treatment.

It is clearly not possible to discuss all the controversies within each individual cancer in a book such as this. First, it would be difficult to remain up to date, as the whole field is changing continually and, second, it may be misleading as there will be minor variations from one centre to another which the reader may perceive as major differences. Nevertheless, there is one particular area of controversy which has been the subject of much of the patient-informed choice work in cancer. This is the management of patients with pre-menopausal breast cancer. There is now a consensus that patients with pre-menopausal breast cancer, who have positive lymph nodes, should undergo adjuvant chemotherapy. Adjuvant simply means treatment in addition to the standard conventional therapy. If the patient had established metastatic disease, then this would simply be the treatment of the disease. With adjuvant therapy, treatment is being given on the assumption that some cells may have passed from the lymph nodes into the blood-stream, and the patient has occult metastatic disease. Adjuvant denotes 'the belt and braces' aspect of this treatment. Adjuvant chemotherapy has been accepted treatment in pre-menopausal breast cancer patients with positive lymph nodes, because of an edict from the National Cancer Institute in the United States. For most oncologists this is no longer controversial. but the problem arises in that no two patients are the same. At what point; how many nodes; at what level are the positive nodes; what is the size of these nodes; and is there any extracapsular spread? These are all questions which will influence the nature of the chemotherapy, the agents to be used, the time for it to be given and even the possibility of bone marrow transplantation. With the resurgence of interest in bone marrow transplantation for breast cancer, the whole area has once again become a minefield. In order to avoid confusion and misunderstanding, it is important that you ask your doctor why a particular course of action has been chosen for you, and on what evidence this decision has been based, and what alternatives might be considered.

MEDIA HYPE

Most days of the week we can pick up a newspaper and find an article in it somewhere on the subject of cancer. Hardly a week goes by without headlines on the television about another break-through in the disease. Many of these should be treated with great caution and a large spoonful of salt. Headlines such as 'Vaccine has 70 per cent success rate in cancer' often break down to the fact that the success was simply the apparent response in patients at risk of a disease, rather than curing a normally terminal disease in 70 per cent of patients. It is unfortunate that, in order to sell newspapers or obtain viewing figures, such stories abound, but that is a fact of life. As a cancer patient, or the relative of a cancer patient, it is important to stay calm, to look at the information which you are given and, if this is inadequate, try to find out more – perhaps through the newspaper or the centre involved in the research. Oncology departments are quite used to having their switchboard jammed the morning after such sensational news. In most instances the news relates to a small sub-group of patients in a particular part of the world, and is not widely applicable and, perhaps more important, not widely available. Rest assured, if a treatment is genuinely effective, it is likely to become widely available relatively quickly. The truth is that much of what is discovered and portrayed as a breakthrough does not stand up to more intensive testing.

CANCER QUACKERY

Oncology is a very specialized field. Clinical oncologists or radiation oncologists, medical oncologists, surgical oncologists, gynaecological oncologists, all deal with cancer every day, and have undergone training over some period of years. Nevertheless, cancer is a relatively common disease, and many other members of the medical profession will also frequently deal with cancer, and in most cases probably very well. But there are dangers in seeking advice from people who set themselves up as experienced and qualified in the field when this is simply not the case. Occasionally, such individuals hit the headlines when their rather unorthodox practice of giving strange hormone injections or other unconventional therapy comes to light. Having had a diagnosis of cancer made, if you have access to the expertise of an oncologist, then this should be sought. There has been much publicity in the UK of late about the poorer cancer survival statistics in comparison with Europe and North America. Some of this can be explained by the poor access to oncologists in the UK, and consequently the mixed bag of treatments which patients may receive. Where there are therapies which are proven gold standard, these are not always being used if the patient is not seen by somebody experienced in the management of their disease. If you feel that your own treatment has been rather unconventional, and you have concerns about it, you should ask your doctor to explain what they are doing. If you are still unhappy and uncertain, then it is reasonable to ask for a second opinion. This has been discussed in Chapter 4.

CHAPTER TWELVE

The Future

BREAKTHROUGHS AND REALITY

Over the last 50 years there have been dramatic improvements in the way in which we treat cancer. The way we practice surgery, radiotherapy and chemotherapy today would not be possible without the considerable research carried out both in the laboratory and at the bedside. As we have seen, cancer is not one disease but many. This has considerable implications for treatment. How can we provide a standard and simple cure for diseases as diverse as breast, lung and colon cancer? Furthermore, it seems as though the mysteries of how to effectively treat some of the commoner cancers are being hidden from us. Whilst there have been tremendous advances and improvements in survival and cure in leukaemia, lymphoma, testicular cancer, choriocarcinoma and, thankfully, children's cancer, many of the common cancers have remained untouched. We often think of cancer research as a war – the war on cancer. If we look at the battlefield, how do the troops stack up?

Well, first there is a lot of cancer research going on worldwide. Different countries have different philosophies about how this is funded. In the United States most cancer research is funded by central government through the National Cancer Institute. Charities such as the American Cancer Society represent only a small component of the total research effort. Individual universities, hospitals and the pharmaceutical industry all contribute to the research effort in North America. In Britain the situation is rather different, with the Government spending a very small amount on cancer research through the Medical Research Council. The cancer charities dominate, with the Imperial Cancer Research Fund being the largest, and the Cancer Research Campaign second in size. Both spend around £50 million annually on cancer research in different ways, and both produce annual reports that are available simply by telephoning the charity. Their numbers are listed at the end of this book. In addition, there are various other charities, such as the Leukaemia Research Fund (specializing in leukaemia research) and the cancer care charities – Cancer Relief Macmillan Fund and the Marie Curie. Understanding how cancer research is funded will help you assess what is going on in this vital area.

We have already referred to media hype and the cancer breakthrough stories which appear in the Press. It may be a new drug, a vaccine, a new form of treatment or a new way to reduce the side-effects of chemotherapy. Why is cancer such a popular topic for breakthrough stories? Well, the simple answer is that there are powerful vested interests at work that tend to keep cancer at the forefront of the news.

Journalists love a good story. If it is fed to them in the right way they are likely to publish it almost as it stands. The cancer charities produce one or two press releases every week, detailing some of their advances. Now, of course, journalists are never known to play down a story – that would not sell papers. So, it is hyped up by the public relations experts – the spin doctors of the cancer charities, responsible for making sure that their charity is well represented in the news. That's what leads to a 'breakthrough' every week.

The major charities act very responsibly in this regard, but some smaller groups – especially companies with a potential anti-cancer product – just before some critical financial episode, such as the sale of shares or a takeover, may act in a highly irresponsible manner, giving false hope to many.

The best advice we can give you is to take it all with a pinch of salt. Of course, there are going to be genuine discoveries which will have considerable impact on medicine, and this chapter outlines where we think they are coming from.

GAZING INTO THE CRYSTAL BALL

There is not likely to be a single breakthrough which will suddenly cure all cancers; it is just not that sort of disease, but there will be a steady improvement. How can you make sure that those professionals responsible for your care are actually getting the latest information about your particular disease? We now live in an age of information technology, an age where news made 12,000 miles away travels within a millisecond on the information superhighway we call the media. And medical information travels fast through orthodox medical channels. Each month there is a considerable increase in our knowledge database on cancer printed in the medical journals. If you pick up the *Lancet*, the *New England Journal of Medicine*, or the *British Journal of Cancer*, you will find a series of papers suggesting new approaches to old problems.

Much of cancer research is aimed at understanding why cells grow and how they go wrong. Some of the research charities are criticized by their donors for being too fundamental in their outlook, but this is where the future is coming from. To understand how to mend a car, we first have to find out how it works. Much of modern cancer research is molecular biology – trying to understand the way in which the various building blocks of cells are made up and interrelate to each other – in other words, finding out how a cell works. We know that somewhere in the intricate control processes of growth and cell division lies the key. It is likely that five or six changes within the DNA of the cell – the thread of life – occur when a cell becomes cancerous. Can these changes be reversed or can ways be found to circumvent the abnormalities they cause? These are the key questions which will lead to the new treatments of the future.

Let us look into the crystal ball at the next 25 years. We will take each of the main three treatment modalities in turn and then consider how our understanding of cancer as a process is likely to improve. Of course, we could be wrong here, but at least it will give a scaffolding on which to base the likely future scenario until the year 2020.

SURGERY

Cancer surgery is an ancient art. Yet, if a tumour was fixed to blood vessels in deeper structures this would have disastrous consequences. Modern cancer surgery began in the nineteenth century when antiseptics and anaesthetics were available, and a basic understanding of how a cancer grew and spread through lymphatics was available.

Conservation became increasingly widespread in cancer surgery, having been helped by modern technology in other areas. Twenty years ago the standard treatment for a bone tumour in the leg of a child was an amputation. We now know that this is not necessary. Technology has helped through new forms of bone grafting. This allows us to give radiotherapy first, followed by excision of the tumour, with bone grafting so that the limb can be spared. As most children with leg tumours are potentially curable, bone grafting has clearly provided a great advance in terms of improvement of quality of life for these children.

The next 10 years is likely to see further conservation in cancer surgery through better technology. New skin grafting techniques with the use of synthetic collagen are helpful in producing better cosmetic results from patients who have surgery for skin cancer, including melanoma. Better ways of reattaching small blood vessels (microsurgery) have also helped in permitting greater conservation throughout cancer surgery.

Another advance we will see over the next 10 years is the impact of keyhole surgery on cancer. Keyhole surgery, as the name implies, involves the use of making a tiny hole through which a flexible operating instrument is passed. The most common area of the body for the use of keyhole surgery is the abdomen using a laparoscope, an instrument which contains a flexible telescope, and tiny surgical instruments which can be manipulated by the operator, sometimes through a computer. Until now, laparoscopic surgery has been limited to relatively simple gynaecological operations, such as cutting off the Fallopian tubes to sterilize women to prevent further pregnancies. But new technology has led to a new style of instrument able to carry out extremely sophisticated surgery. Appendectomy, removal of gall bladder and ovarian cysts, are all now possible through the laparoscope. The main attraction is that the lack of major muscle damage has led to much faster post-operative recovery. Instead of being in hospital for a week after abdominal surgery, patients just need to come in for one night. In some cases, day-case surgery of the abdomen is possible, with the patient going home a few hours afterwards. It is, therefore, not only that the amount of pain and discomfort is much smaller, but the whole procedure can be made less costly. This is attractive to increasingly cost-conscious health care providers, whatever the politics of the system involved. There are several patients with primary colon cancer who have had successful treatment with laparoscopic surgery. Trials are now in progress to make the direct comparison between conventional and keyhole surgery, as this is clearly vital before routinely using this new form of surgery in a widespread manner.

It may be rather horrifying to think of robots performing surgery, but this could well be part of the future scene – for example, for removal of brain tumours. At the moment these are identified by various scans, such as CT or MRI. The data is collected as a mathematical matrix which is subsequently imposed on an X-ray. The radiologist comments on the likely site of a tumour, and the surgeon takes action. Why not connect the mathematical power of the scanning apparatus directly to a robot effector that can remove the tumour using mathematical co-ordinates without human intervention? Brain tumours are a good place to start, as the skull provides fixed co-ordinates around which everything can be calculated. Other parts of the body, such as the abdomen are more difficult, at least for the time being. But it is perfectly feasible that a robotic 'mouse' could be developed to carry out complex operations.

So, what's the surgeon of 2020 going to be like. Well, he or she may be a home worker, working from a computer console while an assistant is actually in the hospital plugging in various minimally invasive devices and robotically controlled sensors with effector arms. The role of the surgeon will be very much to check the diagnosis and then co-ordinate the technology required, which itself will be semi-automatic. Within 20 years the surgical skill of the human hand may well be a throw-back to the past. Instead, tiny robotic devices will be inserted down a flexible tube into the relevant part of the body, and be collected after they have performed their highly programmed tasks. This might sound a little frightening, but the power of the computer in all spheres of activity is here to stay. It can learn to perform better than the humans that built the original machine. Surgery for cancer is, after all, a destructive procedure for the part of the body involved. Anything which can be done to minimize the damage by removing just the tumour and only the smallest amount of normal tissue, so that the tumour will not return, will be an advance.

As we have seen elsewhere in this book, patients don't die from their local disease, they die from its spread – the process of metastasis. This can often be reduced by the use of adjuvant therapy. This simply means treatment given in the absence of any clinical or X-ray evidence that any of the tumour was left behind. The commonest use of adjuvant chemotherapy is in breast cancer. Here, we know that in certain categories of women, those under the age of 50 who have had lymph nodes involved with their cancer under the axilla, there will be a 30 per cent improvement in survival with six months of relatively straightforward chemotherapy. This represents a big advance for this group of patients when we think of the numbers of women involved with this common disease. In future it is likely that more cancer patients will receive adjuvant chemotherapy when we work out which patients would benefit from it most.

One of the problems with adjuvant therapy at the moment is that large numbers of people have chemotherapy in order to benefit only a small sub-group. If we could identify the sub-group in advance, by special tests, it would be even more worth giving. A good example is colon cancer. We know that when the disease has spread through the bowel wall, chemotherapy with 5 fluorouracil, used in conjunction with folinic acid, will prolong survival. In patients where there is no evidence of spread through the bowel wall there seems to be no benefit. Over the next decade, better indicators of the need for adjuvant chemotherapy for colon cancer will be discovered. Instead of the pathologists just commenting on the shape and type of tumour cells, they will also be able to give a much better guide to the need for further treatment by looking at various molecular measurements in the tumour.

LIKELY DEVELOPMENTS IN SURGERY OVER THE NEXT 25 YEARS

1995

- *Increasing conservation: breast, bowel, skin, bone cancers.*

- *New technology:*

  colon staple gun

  minimally invasive surgery

  devices for colon

  novel plastic materials

  laser surgery

- *Adjuvant drug and radiation therapy for high-risk groups; breast and colon.*

2005

- *Training by virtual reality systems.*

- *New minimally invasive devices.*

- *Better tumour imaging.*

- *Distance surgery.*

- *Robotic devices.*

- *New technology: robotics and lasers.*

- *Tailoring adjuvant chemotherapy by molecular markers.*

2020

- *Increased conservation.*

- *Robotic devices appplicable to 2–3 sites – larynx, brain, pelvis.*

- *Distance surgery by computer-aided techniques.*

- *Robotics for many tasks.*

- *Routine virtual reality surgery.*

- *Tailored adjuvant therapy based on individual oncogene/tumour suppressor.*

- *Gene profile.*

- *Ultra conservative internal robotic.*

- *Scarless surgery.*

RADIOTHERAPY

Radiotherapy is a very powerful weapon against cancer. To improve current technology requires two things. The first is our ability to physically direct radiation to the correct place by learning more about where the tumour is, and to make sure the radiation is going there and not to any surrounding normal tissue. The second improvement we need is to increase the selective power of radiation to destroy cancer cells and not normal cells. This can be done by altering the timing with which radiotherapy is given, or by adding other agents (drugs, heat and so on) to selectively increase the killing of cancer cells. Let us now consider each of these in turn and how they fit into the crystal ball for the next 25 years.

Over the last two decades, our ability to visualize tumours using various types of scan has improved dramatically. The process of planning radiotherapy is no longer based on a series of shadows in which the tumour is often imagined with great difficulty. We can now positively identify cancer, and it is logical that over the next 10 years we will increase our ability to define the demarcation line where the cancer ends and normal tissue begins. Identifying this demarcation zone is critical to the planning of precise radiotherapy.

A good example is cancer of the cervix – the neck of the womb. By understanding the exact anatomy of the patient, we can configure precisely the shape of the radiation beam to target the tumour, allowing a margin of 0.5 of a centimetre. No two patients have identically shaped tumours – there are always differences. Furthermore, the normal anatomy differs enormously between different patients. This applies to every type of cancer. So, by making sure we have all the information available about the size and site of the tumour we can use computer technology to ensure that radiation is delivered to the right place. Currently, the radiotherapy volume that we target is usually a geometrically symmetrical shape – for example, a sphere or a brick. But cancers have their own shapes. Actually targeting the radiation to that specific shape by varying the configuration of the beams used is now beginning to be possible, thanks to advanced computer technology. It is called conformal therapy, as the radiation conforms precisely to the shape of the tumour. This technology is likely to improve. Just imagine how much power there is in a simple hand-held child's computer game. Twenty years ago such an apparatus would have filled a large room. In 25 years' time the radiotherapy we give will be much more exact. It is also likely that the planning and delivery phases will not be separate. One machine will identify the site of the tumour and monitor it as it shrinks. The radiotherapy apparatus will compute exactly the best way to configure the field each time the patient comes up for treatment. Information about the anatomy of the patient and other facts that bear on the radiation delivery will be stored on a 'smart card' which will monitor and record exactly what is being done. We can see the beginnings of this technology in the magnetic strip cards that are now used to operate public telephones.

Robotics will also play an important role in the radiotherapy of the future. By understanding more fully the exact geographical location, a combination of conventional external treatment, coupled with new internal sources of radiation, could be used. These internal sources can be 'magic bullets' – such as monoclonal antibodies which are given intravenously, and home in on tumour cells, carrying warheads of radioactive isotope or physically applied tiny tubes or needles which deliver a source directly into the tumour. We already see the use of this technology in the apparatus conventionally used to treat cancer of the cervix today. Here, a tube is placed through the vagina into the cervix (the neck of the womb) and a radioactive source delivered for a short period of time to provide a high dose of radiation just at the point it is needed.

Such physical improvements will almost certainly be helped by improvements in increasing the selectivity of the killing powers of radiotherapy for cancer cells. Just as no two tumours have the same shape, no two tumours have the same biological sensitivity to the harmful effects of radiation. It makes little sense for every patient to have the same dose, and for that dose to be given in the same way. We know that the timing of radiation delivery is also critical to its damaging effect to normal tissue. At the moment, most people receiving radiotherapy for cure of a tumour receive between six to seven weeks of daily treatments, Mondays to Fridays. This type of programme has arisen for logistic reasons, and not because it is necessarily the best for the individual. There is nothing magic in it; it may well be that for certain tumours a short, sharp course of treatment with larger doses per fraction will be better than a long drawn-out course. Similarly, extending the treatment time may be better for other tumours. It is all a matter of selectivity, trying to maximize cancer cell death at the same time as preserving the function of normal tissues. And, of course, different normal tissues may have different sensitivities. To make matters even more complex there is good evidence that the sensitivity of different people varies enormously, so that a complex equation of tumour and normal tissue sensitivity has to be sorted out. It is likely that, over the next five years, new indicators of tumour sensitivity will be found, and over the next 25 a much more detailed programme of differential sensitivity using molecular methods assessed on a regular basis.

By the year 2020 a patient will have a small sample of tumour taken together with a DNA sample from blood, and the two will be examined for radiation sensitivity. A computer will be used to programme exactly how best to maximize the difference when planning how to give the radiation. For some patients this may mean having radiotherapy three times a day for a week. In others it may mean an eight-week course of daily treatment including Saturdays and Sundays. Provided the tumour is localized, it may be possible to maximize the effects of radiation using such a strategy.

As well as learning about the natural sensitivity to radiation of cancer cells in a particular patient, it may be possible to enhance this sensitivity selectively. We already know of various techniques to do this. There are drugs available which are called radiosensitizers. These may be especially effective in cells that lack oxygen. We know that such cells become resistant to the damaging effects of radiation by selectively sensitizing hypoxic cells, which are present in most solid tumours. We may be able to increase the effectiveness of radiation. Extensive clinical trials have been carried out with very limited success because of the toxic, unpleasant side-effects of this group of drugs. It is possible that new drugs will be discovered over the next few years that will be much more effective.

Another radiosensitizer, which is extremely simple, is the use of heat – hyperthermia – heating up tumours to 41°C (106°F). It is an experimental technique that has been used for the last 50 years. Recently, there was a clear-cut demonstration that heating tumours by a few degrees dramatically increases their sensitivity to radiotherapy, but the mechanism of this is not clear. By understanding the mechanism it may be possible to mimic the effects of hyperthermia by using drugs. The main problem with hyperthermia, currently, is the clumsiness with which it can be delivered. Although it is very feasible to heat skin nodules to 41°C (106°F) without causing any problems; deep-seated tumours are a much more difficult technical problem. Research, however, may get round this, and new hyperthermia-based radiation-enhancing systems for clinical use may well emerge. As well as drug and hyperthermia-based radiosensitization, genetic sensitization may well be possible. The basis of radiation sensitivity must be encoded in the DNA of the tumour and normal cells in the patient. It may be possible to selectively switch on increased radiosensitivity just in the cancer cells. It may also be possible to switch off the genes responsible for DNA repair, therefore increasing the destructive effects of radiation on the cancer.

So, in 25 years' time what will the radiotherapist be doing? He or she will be using completely computerized technology to make sure the physical delivery of radiation is correct; genetic information to predict the best way of timing the radiation for that patient; new physical delivery methods to conform to the geography of the tumour, and new ways to enhance the sensitivity of the radiation selectively to the cancer cell. However effective locally, radiation, like surgery, will fail if tumour cells have spread from the confines of the irradiated site. For this reason, some form of systemic therapy – that is, therapy that goes right round the body – will be needed. Chemotherapy and hormone therapy are two such modalities currently in use which will almost certainly be enhanced by the powerful advances in our understanding of the basic biology of cancer.

POTENTIAL ADVANCES IN RADIOTHERAPY OVER THE NEXT 25 YEARS

1995

- *Conformal XRT for certain sites.*

- *Fractionation trials, e.g. CHART.*

- *Radiosensitizers.*

- *Hyperthermia.*

- *Targeted radiation – antibodies.*

2005

- *Conformal therapy – most sites.*

- *Designer fractionation based on molecular assays on tumour and normal tissue.*

- *Routine PET response prediction.*

- *Genetic assays for radiosensitivity.*

- *Radiation response genes cloned.*

2020

- *One-stop planning – therapy.*

- *Computer planning optimization.*

- *Designer fractionation.*

- *Virtual reality tumour images.*

- *Radiation targeting – new tissue-specific ligands (bonded molecule).*

- *Gene therapy – RT using radiation.*

- *Response element (RRE) promoters.*

- *Complete computerization of RT planning.*

- *Robotic set-up of patient.plan – treatment verification at each treatment set-up.*

- *Designer fractionation based on DNA sequence.*

- *Data of tumour and normal tissue.*

- *High affinity specific targeting.*

CHEMOTHERAPY

Chemotherapy is attractive in that drugs can penetrate right round the body, seeking out cancer cells wherever they may be hiding. The real problem, as outlined in Chapter 7, is the very similarity between cancer cells and their normal counterparts. This means that most chemotherapy schedules are toxic, causing serious side-effects. There are many new drugs currently undergoing clinical evaluation. Unfortunately, many of these drugs are based on existing molecules and are unlikely to radically change future treatment. In the screening programmes of the 60s and 70s, new drugs were identified in plants, fungi and bacteria and these produced a number of useful reagents, but they are unlikely to produce many more. The recent excitement about Taxol™, a drug extracted from the bark of the Pacific yew tree, was really based on an observation made in the early 60s, and is nothing drastically new, despite its high public profile. There may well be new drugs on the way, found by empirical discovery, just like Alexander Fleming and penicillin. But, it is more likely that the future of new drug development lies with molecular biology.

By understanding more about growth control and identifying the molecular cogs that make cancer cells tick, better reagents can be designed. Designer anti-cancer drugs are just at their beginning. In the pharmacology laboratory, scientists can take a particular process, such as a growth factor receptor on the surface of a cell, model it using computer graphics and design theoretical compounds that can interfere with its function. These compounds can be synthesized in the organic chemistry laboratory and tested by molecular interactions in systems where there are no living cells. Compounds that work can be enhanced by making chemical modifications to them, then testing them in living cells, and eventually in clinical trials. Most pharmaceutical companies involved in cancer research now have very sophisticated programmes of new drug development. They are based on logical design strategies. It is likely that such developments will lead to the drugs of the future – indeed we could well be entering a 'golden age' of new anti-cancer drug discovery.

POTENTIAL ADVANCES IN CHEMOTHERAPY OVER THE NEXT 25 YEARS

1995

- *New drugs and hormones.*

- *High-dose chemotherapy.*

- *BMT and stem cell rescue.*

- *New antiemetics.*

2005

- *Simulated antibody structures.*

- *Low molecular weight tumour targeting agents.*

- *Radioimmunotherapy.*

- *Toxin targeting.*

- *Antibody fragment gene delivery systems.*

- *Rational cytokine therapy with 'slow release' formulations.*

- *Routine use of genetic vaccines in adjuvant setting.*

2020

- *Routine use of adjuvant immunotherapy.*

- *Cytokine effect prediction.*

- *Novel cytokine discovery.*

- *Immunological resetting after cancer therapy.*

- *Robotic implantation of individualized solid phase multiple cytokine and anti-invasive drug release systems.*

How such drugs will be used, of course, will depend on further clinical investigation. No one could have predicted in the 1940s how chemotherapy was going to turn out. It is similarly difficult to see by the year 2020 how the new drugs of the future will be used. They may well be used in very different ways from those currently in operation. For example, most chemotherapy schedules involve giving drugs at three-weekly intervals. This may well change.

But these are the drugs of the future, and are as yet undiscovered. What can we do to improve current chemotherapy. First, there have been dramatic advances in the reduction of side-effects caused by existing drugs, enabling us to give higher doses. New anti-emetic drugs which stop the sickness and vomiting associated with chemotherapy were first used in the mid–80s and are now universal. Another series of helpful compounds are those that stimulate the bone marrow during chemotherapy. The bone marrow which produces the red and white blood cells as well as platelets (tiny particles which make the blood clot) is very sensitive to the effects of chemotherapy. The reason for this is that bone marrow cells are rapidly dividing, so any drug that prevents cell division will block bone marrow turnover. This can result in serious problems for patients, including infection and bleeding. Factors have been identified called colony stimulating factors, CSFs, which will stimulate turning over of cells in the bone marrow and protect them from the damaging effects of chemotherapy. Cancer cells remain unaffected by these factors. These factors were first identified in the 70s, but only through genetic engineering were they isolated and produced in adequate quantities for clinical trial. These drugs can be given by subcutaneous injection daily, at a time when the blood count is likely to be the lowest, usually from day 5 to day 15 after each cycle of chemotherapy.

Another logical approach to try to escalate the dose of chemotherapy given to patients, without endangering their lives, is to perform an autologous bone marrow transplantation (ABMT). This means removing a patient's bone marrow – it comes from them and is thus autologous – giving the patient a normally lethal dose of chemotherapy, but rescuing them after two or three days with their own bone marrow. This technique has proved to be useful in some patients with non-Hodgkin's lymphoma that are refractory to conventional doses of chemotherapy. It was recently discovered that by giving colony-stimulating factors after a low dose of chemotherapy, some of the bone marrow cells would be released into the peripheral blood and could be collected by filtering them out using a special filtration machine called a plasmapheresis apparatus. Cells could then be stored in the laboratory and given back to the patient after high-dose chemotherapy. This technique, called peripheral blood stem cell grafting (PBSCG), is simpler than bone marrow transplantation and more amenable to development in an out-patient setting, so reducing its cost. There are now extensive trials of PBSCG in breast cancer, especially in those patients who have indicators that they are likely to perform poorly with conventional doses of drugs. An example would be a young woman with extensive lymph node involvement in the axilla after removal of her tumour. Here, the patient is well and there may well be no clinical or X-ray evidence of disease, yet we know statistically that less than 20 per cent of such women will survive more than 10 years. It would, therefore, seem logical to try novel approaches to chemotherapy at an early phase of their illness, rather than wait for the development of recurrence at a later date. It is likely that over the next decade new colony stimulating factors will be found, together with new ways of administering them to optimize their effects. We are anxiously awaiting the results of current trials in breast cancer as a model disease for peripheral blood stem cell grafting that could be applied to other common cancers, including those of the lung, colon, ovary and prostate, if successful.

Another area where new drug development is likely to have a major impact is the process of gene transcription. This is the key to understanding cell behaviour. DNA, the thread of life, is present in every cell. It contains the genes, many of which are switched off. Transcription is the switching process by which a gene is controlled. If it is switched on, a message comes out and protein is made in the cell's protein factory – the ribosome. Until recently, the process of transcription was like a black box. We knew there was a switch but did not really understand how it worked at all. The discovery of transcription factors, tiny molecules which bind to DNA and which decide whether it will allow a gene to be transcribed or not, have proven to be the key to our understanding of the switch process. Some of these transcription factors have turned out to be oncogenes – genes that are mutated or altered in function in cancer cells. It is likely that new drugs will be found which specifically interfere with transcription control, allowing genes to be switched on or off at will.

CANCER GENES

The last 20 years have seen an explosion in our knowledge of the molecular biology of cancer. We now know that there are two families of genes involved. This is a rapidly developing area, and it is likely that over the next five years there will be further great advances. It turns out that there are two sets of genes which determine the state of activity of a normal and cancer cell.

The first are called the oncogenes. These are pieces of DNA which encode for proteins that are involved in the stimulation of growth. These proteins can be likened to the various parts of a car connecting the accelerator pedal to the carburettor. Here, increased petrol/air intake into the cylinder occurs when the pedal is pressed. If these genes are mutated or altered in such a way as to be permanently switched on, then the cell will accelerate, so making it malignant. The second family of cancer genes are those involved in slowing down cellular activity, the tumour suppressors or anti-oncogenes. These products can be likened to the bits of the car connecting the brake pedal to the brake pads at the wheels. Again, when something goes wrong, braking becomes impossible and the cell gradually accelerates. The growth state of a cell is under the continual influence of the products of oncogenes and tumour suppressor genes.

We now know that between 5–6 genetic changes may be necessary for cancer to develop. Figure 12.1 shows, as an example, colon cancer. You can see that there are several genes involved, and the genetic changes in the cells leading to cancer may well be different in each patient. This would explain why colon cancer behaves so differently in different people. By understanding more about oncogenes and tumour suppressor genes and how they interrelate to the natural history and spread of cancer we may begin to make sophisticated molecular predictions about tumour behaviour. This will allow us to tailor the relative aggression of our chemotherapy much more precisely to the needs of an individual.

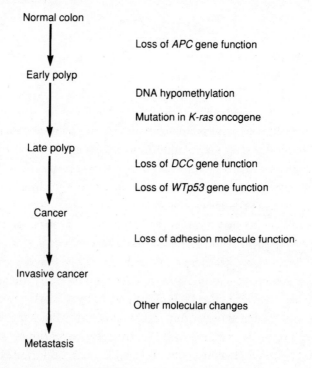

Figure 12.1 *Known molecular abnormalities that lead a normal colon cell down the pathway to cancer.*

How Cells Die

Another area of growing interest in cancer research is the mechanism of why cells die. We tend to think of cancer as a disease caused by increased cell division and the accumulation of accelerating cells. This may not necessarily be so. An alternative way cancer could emerge is if normal cell-death pathways become inactivated. Normal tissue continually turns over – that is, cells die and are replaced by fresh cells. The skin, lungs and the breasts are good examples of such tissue. The process of orderly cell death is called apoptosis. It involves the activation of a set of genes which result in programmed cell destruction. There is evidence that in certain cancer cells the programme is faulty, allowing them to escape death. Recently, the molecular mechanisms of apoptosis have been elucidated and it is likely that new drugs will be developed based on correcting the apoptotic defect found in certain cancer cells.

Metastasis

Clearly, local tumours are amenable to surgery and radiotherapy, and when they spread chemotherapy is needed. For years there have been searches for drugs that block the process of metastasis, either by preventing cells from breaking off from tumours or by preventing cells that have broken off from establishing themselves in other tissues, such as the lungs and liver. There are now several promising new agents coming into clinical trial which may have anti-metastatic potential. Measuring their effects is not straightforward as they may have little or no effect on the size of a primary tumour. Instead, patients have to be carefully selected, given the anti-metastatic drug and followed up to see if the natural history of the tumour with the drug is different from that in a group of patients who are not taking it. Such randomized controlled trials can take a long time to complete, but are vital if we are to discover new agents that work in this way.

IMMUNITY AND CANCER

For many years it has been recognized that in all of us lies a powerful immune response that can recognize cancer cells, either by making antibodies – tiny warheads that combine to cancer cells – or by activating white cells in the body to infiltrate tumours and destroy them through a variety of mechanisms. Over the last few years there has been much activity in understanding how the immune system works and how it relates to cancer. The problem seems to be that cancer cells are clever in producing substances locally which inactivate the soldiers of the immune system. Otherwise, of course, cancer could not emerge in the first place. It may be that under many circumstances the immune system is able to detect and eradicate some early cancers, and this may be part of an on-going process called immunosurveillance. But, once a tumour is established it is difficult to see how a relatively weak immune system could deal with a large and aggressive solid tumour.

Several research strategies are currently in operation to try to enhance the immune response to cancer. These include the administration of genetically engineered cytokines – communication molecules that allow different types of white cell to talk to each other. Such drugs include the interferons, interleukins, tumour necrosis factor and various other proteins which can be given by injection or by infusion to stimulate the immune system to react more strongly against the cancer cells.

Another particularly ingenious method has been to use monoclonal antibodies – 'magic bullets'. These antibodies can be created in an animal or bacteria outside the patient, and can be genetically engineered to make them human in structure. They can be labelled with a warhead which may be a drug, a biological toxin, or a radioactive isotope. After administration, such antibodies can home in on tumour cells carrying their warhead directly to the tumour, destroying it selectively. Clinical trials are in progress to evaluate the true role of monoclonal antibodies. An example at

Hammersmith Hospital is the use of an antibody against ovarian cancer labelled with a radioactive isotope and administered directly into the fluid bathing the abdominal cavity. As ovarian cancer tends to spread first around the abdominal cavity before going elsewhere, it seems logical to try to destroy any free-floating cells in this area first.

Other approaches to harness the immune system involve the cultivation of lymphocytes outside the body, and their administration back to patients. Such adoptive immunotherapy strategies include the use of activated killer cells harvested from blood, and also lymphocytes (white cells) taken directly from the tumour – tumour infiltrating lymphocytes. Responses have been documented by many research groups now for certain cancers, but especially in renal cell cancer and melanoma. It is likely that as we more fully understand the immune system and how it operates we will be able to devise more targeted approaches to dealing with cancer using immune stimulants.

GENE THERAPY

As you will now appreciate, cancer is a disorder of genes, the genes that control growth apparatus of the cell. Doctors and scientists have recently been able to manipulate pieces of DNA, inserting them at the correct points so that they functionally express their message and subsequently protein. The burgeoning science of gene therapy is now being applied to many fields in medicine, from congenital disorders such as the 'boy in the bubble' syndrome, through to inherited diseases such as cystic fibrosis. The new genetics is promising tremendous advances in therapy. So, too, in cancer where there is the possibility of correcting the very basis of the disease. What does gene therapy mean, practically, and how long will it be before it can be successfully applied? Already 200 patients have been studied worldwide, and some interesting results have been observed. But, at the moment, it is just an experimental tool, as few of the patients have benefited from being included in the trials. Gene therapy has caught the imagination of many – journalists, doctors, scientists and the public. Let us look at its possibilities for cancer patients.

There are many approaches using gene therapy for cancer. The first to enter extensive clinical trial is the modification of the immune response. In the previous section we examined the immune response to cancer, and that often it is very weak. If we could somehow manipulate cancer cells to make them more easily seen by the body's immune system, then it may just be possible that the patient's immune system will do the job of getting rid of the cancer. This is the strategy that is being applied now to a variety of tumours, especially those known to cause a relatively strong immune stimulus, such as melanoma and renal cell cancer. A piece of tumour is taken from the patient surgically, and minced up. A suspension of cells is then made. An immune-stimulating gene, such as Interleukin 2 or tumour necrosis factor inserted into an artificial virus, is then allowed to infect tumour cells in the laboratory. The cells are then irradiated to stop them replicating, and are given back to the patient as a vaccine. The idea is that the tumour cells will now secrete a little cloud of immune-activating molecules, so attracting a large number of the patient's white cells which will be stimulated to recognize the tumour. This type of technique is called genetic immunomodulation.

Another approach which is of considerable interest is the insertion of suicide genes into cancer cells. Here, a virus is used to infect the cancer cells directly in a patient, either by direct injection into the tumour or through the bloodstream. The trick is to use a small molecular switch in the virus, artificially created by the scientist, and which is only switched on in cancer cells. This in turn switches on an enzyme which can convert a normally harmless drug into a very active chemotherapy agent (*see Figure 12.2*). There are many potential molecular switches and many potential drug-activating systems. It is likely that over the next five years we will hear a lot about selectively targeted chemotherapy using genetic switching. The attraction here is that not every cancer cell

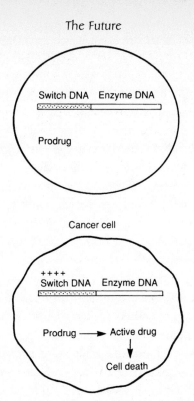

Figure 12.2 Gene therapy for cancer, using a drug-activating gene.

needs to be infected with the virus or artificial genetic vehicle. There is a bystander effect, so that if one tumour cell out of 10 produces the enzyme, then all its neighbours may well die because of the release of the active drug.

The future of gene therapy may well be in trying to correct the very basis of the cancer. Repairing the defective brakes of the cell – the tumour suppressor genes – or down-regulating any aberrant accelerator molecules, the oncogenes, could well be feasible in 10 years' time. The problem at the moment is that every cancer cell would have to have its genetic defect corrected. Even a single cell remaining uncorrected will grow up to form a new tumour in the patient. Currently, we just don't have the ability to make sure every cell is targeted. But gene therapy has a great future.

CANCER PREVENTION AND SCREENING

As well as health education improvements, it is likely that new screening techniques will be used to help prevent cancer or at least to detect it at a pre-malignant stage. Such techniques are likely to be based heavily on molecular genetics. A good example is the discovery last year of the gene associated with breast cancer – the BRCA1 gene. Although relatively rare in the population as a whole, there are certain families that have a very high incidence of breast cancer, with nearly all the female members developing the disease. Some of the women in these families also have ovarian cancer. The development of cancer is associated with a change in the BRCA1 gene which, through a mechanism as yet not understood, leads to the development of cancer. It is likely that over the next few years many similar genes will be uncovered. Some of these will be common in a population. DNA testing could then allow prediction of the development of cancer in an individual. One can then imagine that by the year 2010, when the whole sequence of the human DNA has been identified, it may be possible to have a test at the age of 18 which will predict the chances of specific cancers. If, for example, you have a 90 per cent chance of getting breast cancer, then appropriate screening methods can be planned to make sure that it is picked up at the earliest possible stage. If a man has a 95 per cent chance of developing prostate cancer by the age of 60, then one would consider radiotherapy or surgery to the prostate a few years prior to this. Although this, today, may seem like science fiction, the genetic prediction of cancer risk will become a reality. It will almost certainly create all sorts of difficulties for life assurance companies but if we can harvest the information to the advantage of our patients we may be able to prevent the disastrous consequences of metastatic cancer in many, so changing the course of their lives.

QUALITY OF LIFE

Since the Second World War we have seen great changes in the quality of life of everybody, not just cancer patients. We now expect to be well-fed, well-clothed, and most people have either a car or access to one. Things were very different in the 1950s when rationing was still in place. Most of us lived without television, telephones or motor cars. Today, society places a lot of emphasis on quality, and most people are willing to pay for it. A good example might be a cup of coffee at a railway station in Britain. In the 50s this would be cheap and cheerful but not very good. In the 90s our railway stations feature small coffee boutiques where for £1 or so one can obtain a delicious cappuccino.

This simple example also applies to cancer treatment. People are no longer willing to put up with rushed, hurried care in a poor-quality environment and being kept waiting endless hours in draughty hospital corridors. In Britain, with a nationalized health service, it is the Government that has to pay to improve the quality of care through central taxation. In other health systems it is the insurer or individual who pays. Over the next 20 years we are likely to see a further increase in the quality of care that people expect. This is not just technical quality, but also other aspects, such as better daycare facilities for patients receiving chemotherapy, and a faster streamlined diagnostic process to take the worry out of the early stages of cancer so that a definite treatment plan can be obtained within a few days rather than within a few weeks, as at present. Britain's hospitals still often seem to work for their own benefit and not for the benefit of the consumer. The cancer patient needing a series of tests may have to make many visits to the hospital, waiting in different corridors each time to get the necessary package of X-rays and test results together, so that a decision about treatment can be made. If things were better organized this would not need to happen. A single day's visit should be enough for all the investigations required to be conducted in a properly co-ordinated manner.

PSYCHOLOGICAL CARE

As well as the physical quality of life there is also the psychological quality. A lot more effort is now being put into improving communication with cancer patients through courses for medical students, doctors and other health care professionals, and also into learning from those in complementary medicine who have always been much better at being patient-centred in their approach. The Cancer Help Centre at Bristol, in the UK, has provided a great inspiration to many of us in the orthodox world about communication with patients. Allowing people to express their feelings, being a good listener, and responding with empathy are all part of the consultation process and part of the skill of providing high-quality care.

As we go through the next decade, new drugs will probably be discovered to help control mood. Today we have antidepressants, and it is likely that by the turn of the century there will be more powerful, specific mood control agents that can be used for a patients facing different situations. Coupled with good communication skills, such changes will certainly help in dealing with the mood swings many cancer patients have as they come to terms with their disease.

HOW TO GET THE BEST POSSIBLE CARE

One of the biggest problems in cancer treatment, is how best to use the resources we have. Ideally, all hospitals should have some form of cancer treatment service, and this is true to some extent. But, at a time when treatment is changing, it makes good sense to concentrate expensive resources in such a way that all can benefit from them. One way of doing this is to create cancer centres, usually in large towns associated with a university medical school. This means that the cancer centre benefits from the research and teaching atmosphere in which ideas can be questioned and discussed and novel research programmes instigated.

The problem then becomes how to get the patient to the centre. Different countries have come up with different solutions, depending on their geography and health care system. In Canada, for example, a very cohesive group of Government-funded cancer centres have been established, linked to sizeable general hospitals from which patients are rapidly referred once the diagnosis has been made. In the US the situation is more complex – but again there are designated cancer centres which are accredited using objective criteria by the Health Department. In France a network of 20 main units exist, with around 40 smaller subsidiary hospitals providing a more limited service which is centrally monitored.

In Britain the situation is currently haphazard. Pockets of excellence juxtapose with a very poor standard of care. In Scotland, for example, an almost ideal situation has arisen – driven by geography rather than deliberate planning. Four cancer centres – Edinburgh, Glasgow, Aberdeen and Dundee – provide the main treatment bases, with specialists going out to clinics at surrounding general hospitals on a weekly basis. In England the position is rather different. There are over 50 centres involved in cancer treatment which have radiotherapy facilities. Expertise in some of the smaller centres is very limited, and yet patients are only infrequently referred from them to the larger centres. Few doctors like to admit that they are unable to cope with a specific cancer type. Of course, going to a larger centre means inconvenience and disturbance, especially for patients not used to travelling. We badly need better organization in the provision of cancer services in England. There are many political problems in getting this. No politician wants to stand idly by whilst a small cancer unit is closed. For this reason, several attempts to rationalize cancer services in London have failed.

But things are changing rapidly for two reasons. The first is the separation of the NHS into health care purchasers and providers, together with the emergence of a managed market – with an element of competition. The purchasers can insist on certain criteria when placing contracts to buy cancer care for their patients. These can include levels of expertise, equipment and so on. If these are not met their patients can be sent elsewhere. The second reason for change is the setting up of an Expert Advisory Group on Cancer by the Department of Health. This group, chaired by the Chief Medical Officer personally, has produced a new framework for the organization of cancer care – a sort of national cancer plan.

It involves the construction of a three-tier structure: primary care in the GP's surgery; cancer units in sizeable general hospitals and cancer centres at major teaching hospitals. All three levels will be linked. The cancer units will have staff visiting from the centre on a weekly basis and will give chemotherapy. Specialist nurses will be always available to help with problems and, if necessary, refer the patient to the centre immediately. In this way each patient should have access to a high standard of care which can take in rapidly any advances in treatment.

This plan is going to take at least three years to set up. For the time being, how can you make sure you are getting the best?

It is very difficult to put together a 'Good Cancer Treatment Guide' because there are so many factors involved. For example, an elderly person with a small and easily curable skin cancer may be treated just as well in a small and relatively poorly equipped centre. But, for more complex treatment the facilities and expertise available may be totally inadequate. We have put together some of the features of a good centre, so you at least have something to go by. But if you are worried about anything it is most important that you ask to see the consultant and discuss things.

A GOOD CANCER CENTRE ...

- is part of a major hospital with full back-up facilities in many specialities

- is involved in the teaching of doctors, nurses, physicists and radiographers about cancer treatment

- *is carrying out research to assess new cancer treatments*

- *has adequate radiotherapy facilities, including two or more linear accelerators, a simulator and full planning computer facilities*

- *has specialists in medical oncology (chemotherapy and haematology (blood diseases) on its staff*

- *has counselling, palliative care and complementary medicine services to help you if you wish.*

Conclusion

Changes in the management of cancer have been dramatic in the past decade. This has not always been coupled with improved outcome. Nevertheless, greater public awareness and under-standing, better knowledge of the biology of the disease, and advances in the techniques available for investigating and treating cancer, all hold great promise for the future. We believe that these are optimistic times for cancer patients and their families. Our aim in writing this book was to take readers through the cancer disease process, through the treatment and finally on to the prospects for the treated patient. Progress is not simply about prognosis, it is also about a cultural change in the attitude of doctors and paramedical staff. As a result, there should be an under-standing of the need for unbiased information, greater sensitivity to patients' quality of life and, perhaps above all, the right to be involved in decisions about their management. We hope that this book will empower them in that process.

Useful Information

SUPPORT SERVICES

These are mainly for the UK – similar organizations exist in many other countries. Please enquire at your cancer treatment centre for details, as no international directories exist.

BACUP (British Association of Cancer United Patients)
3 Bath Place, Rivington Street, London EC2A 3JR
Cancer information service freeline: 0800 181199
Cancer counselling 0171-696 9000
Information, counselling, leaflets.

Breast Cancer Care
15/19 Britten Street, London SW3 3TZ
Helpline: 0171-867 1103
Freeline: 0500 245345
Breast cancer information, prosthesis advice, counselling.

British Colostomy Association
15 Station Road, Reading, Berks RG1 1LG
01734 391537
Information and advice to colostomy patients.

Cancerlink
7 Britannia Street, London WC1X 9JN
Information service: 0171-833 2451
Asian language: 0171-713 7867
Young people's line: 0800 591028
Information, leaflets, support groups.

Carers National Association
20–25 Glasshouse Yard, London EC1A 4JS
0171-490 8898
Information, leaflets, lobby groups.

Hodgkin's Disease Association
PO Box 275, Haddenham, Aylesbury, Bucks HP17 8JJ
01844 291500
Information and support for patients with lymphoma.

Hospice Information Service
St Christopher's Hospice
51–59 Lawrie Park Road, London SE26 6DZ
0181-778 9252
Details of hospice services in UK and Eire.

The Leukaemia Care Society
14 Kingfisher Court, Venny Bridge, Pinhoe, Exeter, Devon EX4 8JN
01392 464848
Information and financial assistance for leukaemia patients.

Malcolm Sargent Cancer Fund for Children
14 Abingdon Road, London W8 6AF
0171-937 4548
Grants and holidays for children with cancer.

National Association of Laryngectomee Clubs
Ground Floor, 6 Rickett Street, Fulham, London SW6 1RU
0171-381 9963
Information and advice on speech aids, local clubs.

The Neuroblastoma Society
41 Towncourt Crescent, Petts Wood, Kent BR5 1PH
01689 873338
Information and advice on neuroblastoma.

Oesophageal Patients Association
16 Whitefields Crescent, Solihull, West Midlands B91 3NU
Information, advice, visits.

Retinoblastoma Society
Paediatric Oncology, St Bartholomew's Hospital, London EC1A 7BE
0171-600 3309
Advice and help for families.

Tak Tent
Western Infirmary, 20 Western Court, 100 University Place, Glasgow G12 6SQ
0141-211 1932
Information, support group network across Scotland.

Tenovus Cancer Information Centre
142 Whitchurch Road, Cardiff CF4 3NA
0800 526527
Emotional support, information, counselling for people in Wales.

Urostomy Association
Buckland, Beaumont Park, Danbury, Essex CM3 4DE
01245 224294
Counselling–technical help.

Women's National Cancer Control Campaign
Suna House, 128–130 Curtain Road, London EC2A 3AR
0171-729 2229
Breast screening and other information.

COMPLEMENTARY MEDICINE

The Cancer Help Centre
Grove House, Cornwallis Grove, Clifton, Bristol BS8 4PG
0117 9743216
Holistic programme, day and residential courses.

Institute for Complementary Medicine
PO Box 194, London SE16 1Q2
Lists of complementary practitioners.

Royal London Homoeopathic Hospital
Great Ormond Street, London WC1 3HR
0171-837 3091
Holistic programmes, homoeopathy.

Anthroposophical Society in Great Britain
Rudolf Steiner House, 35 Park Road, London NW1 6XT
0171-723 4400
Anthroposophical medicine information.

Association of Hypnotists and Psychotherapists
12 Cross Street, Nelson, Lancs BB9 7EN
01282 699378
Hypnosis and psychotherapy information.

British Medical Acupuncture Society
67–69 Chancery Lane, London WC2A 1AF
Acupuncture information.

British Wheel of Yoga
1 Hamilton Place, Boston Road, Sleaford, Lincs
01529 306851
Lists of yoga and meditation teachers.

Matthew Manning Healing Centre
39 Abbeygate Street, Bury St Edmunds, Suffolk
01284 769502
Healing centre of excellence.

National Federation of Spiritual Healers
Old Manor Farm Studio, Church Street, Sunbury-on-Thames, Middx TW16 6RG
019327 83164
Lists of spiritual healers.

National Institute of Medical Herbalists
PO Box 3, 41 Hatherley Road, Winchester, Hants. SO22 6RR
01962 68776
Herbal information.

INSURANCE PROBLEMS

Agencies that can help with difficulties in obtaining insurance, life assurance or mortgages:

Impaired Lives Insurance Bureau
Trevone House, Pannells Court, Guildford, Surrey GU1 4EY
01483 575282

Association of British Insurers
51 Gresham Street, London EC2V 7HQ
0171- 600 3333

UK CANCER CHARITIES

Predominantly research:

Imperial Cancer Research Fund (ICRF)
44 Lincoln's Inn Fields, London WC2A 3PX
0171-242 0200
Cancer research from laboratory to clinical, through its own research laboratories in London and through units attached to major teaching hospitals around the country. Integrates rapidly advancing information from molecular biology with clinical research in hospitals.

Cancer Research Campaign (CRC)
2 Carlton House Terrace, London SW1Y 5AR
0171-930 8972
Cancer research through either its three major institutes (at the Royal Marsden and Christie Hospitals, and the Beatson Institute in Glasgow) together with research grants to investigators at many UK hospitals and universities.

Leukaemia Research Fund (LRF)
43 Great Ormond Street, London WC1N 3JJ
0171-405 0101
Leukaemia research in various hospials around the UK.

Predominantly care:

Cancer Relief Macmillan Fund
Anchor House, 15–19 Britten Street, London SW3 3TZ
0171-351 7811
Services for palliative care through nurses and doctors integrated throughout NHS system.

Marie Curie Cancer Care
28 Belgrave Square, London SW1X 8QG
0171-235 3325
Nursing care for patients either at home or in hospices.

BEREAVEMENT

The Compassionate Friends
53 North Street, Bristol BS3 1EN
0117 9539639
Self-help group of parents helping those who have lost a son or daughter (any age, including adults).

Cruse
126 Sheen Road, Richmond TW9 1UR
0181-332 7227
Bereavement counselling.

POLITICAL LOBBY

National Cancer Alliance
PO Box 579, Oxford OX4 1LP
01865 793566
New alliance between patients, carers and professionals formed to lobby for better provision for cancer care in the UK.

INTERNATIONAL

American Cancer Society
1599 Clifton Road NE, Atlanta, Georgia 30329, USA
404 320 3333

National Cancer Institute (USA)
Building 31, Room 10A24, 9000 Rockville Pike, Bethesda, Maryland 20892, USA
301 496 5583
Toll free USA 1 800 CANCER

Australian Cancer Society
153 Dowling Street, Woolloomooloo, NSW 2011, Australia
02 358 2066

Canadian Cancer Society
10 Alcorn Avenue, Suite 200, Toronto, Ontario M4V 3B1, Canada
416 961 7223

Irish Cancer Society
5 Northumberland Road, Dublin 4, Eire
01 668 1855

Ulster Cancer Foundation
40–42 Eglantine Avenue, Belfast BT9 6DX
Helpline: 0232 663439

Cancer Society of New Zealand
PO Box 12145, Wellington, New Zealand
04 473 6409

Further Reading

CANCER PREVENTION

Cancer Risks and Prevention, M. Vessey and M. Gray, Oxford Medical Publishers, Oxford, 1985.
Rather dry but informative text on cancer prevention strategies.

Can You Avoid Cancer, Peter Goodwin, BBC Books, London, 1984.
Good summary – easy to read.

Cancer: How to Reduce Your Risks, Heath Education Authority Guide, London, 1993.
Excellent free pamphlet on reducing cancer risk.

CONVENTIONAL

Challenging Cancer from Chaos to Control, Nira Kfir and Maurice Slevin, Routledge, London, 1991.
Unusual book written by a psychotherapist and an oncologist. Fairly high-brow approach – not for everybody.

Breast Cancer – a Guide for Every Woman, Michael Baum, Christobel Saunders and Sheena Meredith, Oxford Paperbacks, Oxford, 1994.
By far the best book on the subject. Clear, easy to read and packed with information.

An Introduction to Psycho-oncology, Patrice Guex, Routledge, London, 1994.
Excellent summary of mind body interactions related to cancer.

Cancer – Your Life, Your Choice, Rachel Clyne, Thorsons, Wellingborough, 1989.
Informative and all embracing – clearly written.

Living with Cancer, Jenny Bryan and Joanna Lyall, Penguin Health, London, 1987.
A little dated, but an excellent and readable book. Still highly recommended.

Having Cancer and How to Live With It, Angela Wilkie, Hodder and Stoughton, London, 1993.
Readable account appealing mainly to women. More about dealing with feelings than explaining medical technology,

Stress, Distress and Illness, Ian Hislop, McGraw-Hill Books, New York, 1991.
A fascinating account of stress and its effects on someone with serious illness, not just cancer.

The Good Doctor Guide, Martin Page, Simon and Schuster, London, 1993.
A controversial list of 'good doctors' in London, including those involved in cancer care. The regulatory authorities hated it, but it's a taste of things to come.

The Diagnosis is Cancer, Edward Larschan and Richard Larschan, Bull Publishing, Palo Alto, USA, 1986.
A useful guide to 'working the system' in the USA. Needs updating.

Helpful Essential Links to Palliative Care – HELP, A.M. Abdel-Fattah and others, Cancer Relief Macmillan Fund, London, 1992.
A useful practical guide to palliative care, mainly for doctors and nurses, but carers could find it useful.

COMPLEMENTARY

Choices in Healing, Michael Lerner, MIT Press, Cambridge, MA, USA, 1994.
Superb review of complementary and alternative techniques. Non-judgemental and packed with information. Excellent value.

Loving Medicine, Rosy Thomson, Gateway Books, Bath, 1989.
Good introduction to the 'gentle approach' with case histories. Holistic approach well explained.

Return of the Rishi, Deepak Chopra, Houghton Mifflin, Boston, USA, 1991.
The mysteries of Ayurvedic healing explained. A bit too American!

New Approaches to Cancer, Shirley Harrison, Century Paperbacks, London, 1987.
Good but rather dated guide to complementary and alternative cancer treatments.

Gentle Giants, Penny Brohn, Century, London, 1986.
The story of a personal journey of a remarkable woman with breast cancer who was co-founder of The Cancer Help Centre, Bristol.

A Cancer Therapy – Results of 50 Cases, Max Gerson, Totality Books, New York, USA,1958.
The essentials of the Gerson Diet presented as anecdotes – an extremist's view.

A True Cancer Cure, S.J. Haught, Major Books, Canoga Park, 1976.
A glowing and uncritical account of the Gerson therapy.

The Bristol Programme, Penny Brohn, Century, London, 1987.
The original Bristol way. Now practised in a modified manner. A good introduction to complementary therapies, but a little extreme on the diet.

Glossary

Biopsy A sample of tissue which is suspicious and can be looked at under the microscope in order to diagnose the condition, which may be the presence or absence of cancer.

Benign Non-cancerous, the opposite of malignant.

Cancer A general term for about 200 different diseases in which the growth of cells proceeds in an uncontrolled fashion and then may spread to other parts of the body which may ultimately result in the death of the individual. All cancers are malignant.

Carcinogen A substance which causes cancer and is usually found in the environment. It may be natural or man-made and can cause, or play a part in, the development of cancer.

Carcinoma A cancer which develops from epithelial cells. These are present in surfaces covering both the outside and inside of the body – skin, lungs, gastrointestinal tract and urinary tract. This is the commonest type of cancer.

Chemotherapy Treatment with drugs, which may be taken by mouth or through a vein, and which destroys cells which are dividing frequently. This affects malignant or cancerous cells in particular. It is often termed cytotoxic, which refers to the ability to kill cells.

Gene A piece of genetic material, deoxyribonucleic acid (DNA), which resides in the nucleus of the cell and codes for a particular function of the cell.

Gene therapy Treatment which involves altering the function of a gene or genes in some way to enable cancer cells to be destroyed, either by an external treatment or the body's own immune system.

Health The World Health Organization has defined health as a state of 'complete physical, mental and social well-being and not merely the absence of disease and infirmity'.

Immunotherapy The treatment of cancer with agents which exist naturally as part of the immune system. The aim is to enhance the body's own defence mechanisms against cancer so that cancer cells are recognized as foreign and eliminated.

Lymphoma A cancer which has arisen in the lymphatic system.

Malignant Cancerous.

Metastasis (secondaries) The spread of cancer from one part of the body to another. The new site in which the cancer cells grow is a metastasis or secondary deposit.

Monoclonal antibodies (magic bullets) Artificially engineered protein molecules which are intended to home in on cancer cells specifically to destroy them.

Oncologist A specialist involved in the treatment of cancer.

Palliative treatment Treatment aimed at the relief of symptoms and improvement of quality of life and not of cure.

Prognosis The medical opinion of the predicted outcome of a person's remaining expectation of life. This is necessarily an estimate and can obviously never be completely accurate.

Radiation The energy given out or emitted by a radioactive substance or machines which produce X-rays.

Radiotherapy The treatment of cancer with X-rays of high energy, usually gamma-rays.

Radiosensitive A cancer which responds to radiation, i.e. is sensitive to it.

Radioresistant A cancer which does not respond to radiation, i.e. is resistant to it.

Remission A state in which there is no evidence of cancer in the body, although this may not mean a cure.

Sarcoma A cancer which has developed in the body's supporting tissues, such as bone, cartilage, muscle, fat and tendons and the tissue between organs (mesenchyme).

Screening The process of looking for a cancer, within the at-risk population, at an early stage when it is more curable.

Staging The assessment of a patient using X-rays, scans etc., to detect how far a tumour has progressed and how widespread it is. This may relate to the stage of the primary tumour itself (T stage) or the presence of nodal (N stage) or metastatic disease (M stage). The extent of most tumours is described by an internationally recognized staging system known as the TNM classification (Tumour, Nodes, Metastasis).

Stoma The diversion of a section of bowel or the ureter (the tube between the bladder and kidney) to the body surface by surgery then opens into a stoma. This allows a bodily function which may otherwise be blocked or where the bladder or the terminal part of the bowel has been removed.

Tumour A swelling or mass of tissue in any part of the body which may be cancerous or benign.

Virus A minute single-cell organism which is only able to multiply by getting into the body's cells and using the genetic material inside that cell. When new viruses are made they are then released from the cell.

Index

acupuncture 140
AIDS 41, 43
alcohol 32, 33
alternative medicine
    see complementary
    medicine
anaemia 115
anaesthetic 64
analgesics 164, 166–7
anti-inflammatory 165
antioxidants 152
atom bombs 36, 37

Bach flower remedies 150
BACUP 143, 161
beer 29
benign tumours 7
  see also tumours
bereavement 168, 172–4
  reaction 173
biopsy 61, 63, 65, 71
blood tests 73, 109, 116, 158
breakthroughs 185–7
breast awareness 50
breast cancer screening 39, 47,
    48

breast reconstruction 87
Bristol Cancer Help Centre
    139, 212
Bristol Diet 151

cancer
  centres 98, 127, 128, 179, 180,
    212, 214–5
  charities 142
  chemicals and 16, 21, 22
  in childhood 128, 121–3, 185
  classification of 11
  genes and 18, 19, 203–4
  hereditary 20
  hormones and 44–5
  immunity and 206–7
  incidence of 18
  occupation and 16
  personality 144, 148, 149
  prevention 210
  risk of 20, 27, 35, 40, 44, 46,
    56–60
  sex and 43
  of specific sites:
    bone 11, 87
    breast 19, 28, 83–6

cervix 41, 43, 44, 47, 193, 194

colon 10, 19, 52, 66, 86–7

head and neck 153

liver 32

lung 12, 22, 23, 24, 53, 61

mouth 32, 36

oesophagus 32, 153

ovary 124, 125

penis 44

prostate 10

skin 34

stomach 153

testicular 17, 53, 123–4

thyroid 37

uterus (womb) 134

Cancerlink 161

carcinogens 29

cell cycle 74

cells 4–8, 106, 156

centres of excellence 76

check-list 55, 78, 81, 91, 99, 134

chemotherapy 14, 71, 74, 111–30, 198–203

adjuvant 182, 190–91

administration 119

side-effects 115–19

nausea and vomiting 117–19

types:

adriamycin (doxorubicin) 115, 119, 125, 150

alkylating agents 111, 114

bleomycin 116

etoposide 123

platinum-compounds 114, 115, 116, 127

taxol 150

vinca alkaloids 112, 121, 125

choriocarcinoma 124

clinical trials 129–30, 179–80

colostomy 86, 160

complementary medicine 137–55

convalescence 89

counselling 137, 140, 142–4

CT scan (Computerized Tomography) 66, 67, 72, 90, 95, 189

cytokines 206–7

diagnosis 61–8, 72, 78

diet 28–31, 154

dietary treatments 151–4

Bristol Diet 151

DNA, deoxyribonucleic acid 5, 6, 7, 8, 34, 37, 93, 112, 113, 187, 195, 202, 207

drug resistance 124–6

drugs 112, 113–15, 125

dying and bereavement 168, 170–71

endocrine gland 132

exercise 46

extremists 141

family history 18, 19

fat 28

finances 159, 171
free radicals 152
follow-up 108, 156, 157–8

gamma rays 34
gene therapy 207–9
general practitioner (family
    doctor) 47, 62, 75, 76, 80,
    109, 142, 159, 177
Gerson Centre (Clinic) 139, 152
glandular fever 42
grade 74

hair loss 106–7, 115
healing 147–8
heat 34
Hepatitis B 42
herbal medicine 150
Hodgkin's disease 120–21, 124
homoeopathy 149
hormone therapy 14, 131–4
  side-effects 133
hospice movement 169–70
humanist 147
hypnotherapy 148

immune system 206–7, 208
infertility 103, 122
interferon *see* cytokines

Kaposi's sarcoma 41

leukaemia 112, 121–3
life insurance 161
light 34

lumpectomy 84, 85
lymphoma 41, 111, 112, 120
  Burkitt's lymphoma 42

magic bullets *see* monoclonal
    antibodies
Magnetic Resonance Imaging
    (MRI) 67, 72, 90, 189
malaria 42
mammography *see* breast
    cancer screening
mastectomy 83
medical oncologist 71
medical oncology 126–8
meditation 145–6
melanoma 35
mesothelioma 21
metastasis 8, 83, 190
monoclonal antibodies 206–7
morphine 165

nausea, with chemotherapy
    118–19

obesity 47
occupational cancers 16, 21
oncogenes 204
oncologist 71–2
operation 87–9, 91

pain control 164–6, 168
pathology 65
patient-informed choice 180
physicist 96, 178
planning 96–7

plastic surgery 89
pregnancy 39
psychological care 212

quality of life 211

radiation 36–40, 94
radioactive source 94, 98
radiographer 96
radiosensitizer 196
radiotherapist 71
radiotherapy 14, 71, 74, 84,
    92–110, 177–9, 193–8
  advice 101
  cosmetic effects 105
  limitations 106
  myths 106
  planning 192
  schedules 179
  sensitivity 102
  side-effects 102–6, 163
receptor 132
recurrence 162
reflexology 140
relaxation 144–5
retinoblastoma 18

sarcoma 10
screening 48, 52–3, 55, 210
  in cancer of the cervix 48
  see also breast cancer
    screening
second opinion 79
self-examination 47, 49, 54
self-healing 138

self-help 143
sex and cancer 42, 43
Simonton technique 148
smoking 22, 23, 24, 47
specialist 72, 74, 76, 127
staging 73–7
sunshine 34
support groups 137, 161,
    216–18
surgeon 71
  orthopaedic 87
surgery 13, 71, 82–91, 188–92
  keyhole 188–9
survival curves 157
symptoms 12–15, 61
systemic disease 111

tamoxifen 133
TNM classification 73
treatment 13, 74, 129
tumour 7–8
  flare 133

ultrasound 67
ultraviolet light 34–5

vegan 141
viruses 40–43
visualization 146–7

work 158–9

x-rays 34, 36, 38, 39, 47, 92, 94,
    158
x-ray investigations 65, 66, 189